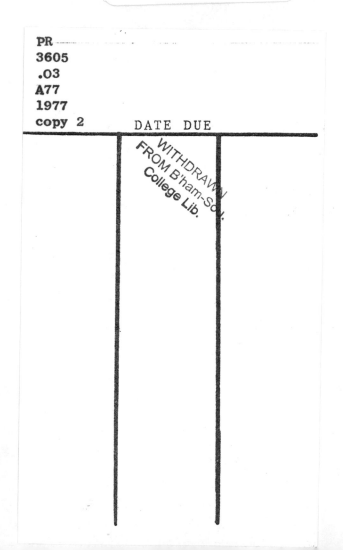

WILD OATS

THE HEREFORD PLAYS
General Editor E. R. Wood

Robert Ardrey
Thunder Rock

Maxwell Anderson
Winterset

Robert Bolt
A Man for All Seasons
The Tiger and the Horse
Vivat! Vivat Regina!

Harold Brighouse
Hobson's Choice

Coxe and Chapman
Billy Budd

Gordon Daviot
Dickon

Barry England
Conduct Unbecoming

George Farquhar
The Recruiting Officer

J. E. Flecker
Hassan

Ruth and Augustus
Goetz
The Heiress

H. Granville-Barker
The Voysey Inheritance

(Ed.) E. Haddon
Three Dramatic Legends

Willis Hall
The Long and the Short and the Tall

Fritz Hochwalder
The Strong are Lonely

Henrik Ibsen
The Master Builder
An Enemy of the People

D. H. Lawrence
The Widowing of Mrs Holroyd and *The Daughter-in-Law*

Roger MacDougall
Escapade

Arthur Miller
The Crucible
Death of a Salesman
All My Sons
A View from the Bridge

Bill Naughton
Spring and Port Wine

André Obey
Noah

J. B. Priestley
An Inspector Calls
Time and the Conways
When We Are Married
Eden End
The Linden Tree

James Saunders
Next Time I'll Sing to You
A Scent of Flowers

R. C. Sherriff
Journey's End

J. M. Synge
The Playboy of the Western World and *Riders to the Sea*

David Storey
In Celebration
The Changing Room

Brandon Thomas
Charley's Aunt

Peter Ustinov
Romanoff and Juliet

John Whiting
Marching Song
Saint's Day
A Penny for a Song
The Devils

Oscar Wilde
The Importance of Being Earnest

Tennessee Williams
The Glass Menagerie

WILD OATS

or

THE STROLLING GENTLEMEN

A Comedy in
Five Acts
by

JOHN O'KEEFFE

The text as prepared and directed by
CLIFFORD WILLIAMS
for the Royal Shakespeare Company
with an Introduction and
Editorial Material by
the Director

HEINEMANN EDUCATIONAL BOOKS

LONDON

Heinemann Educational Books Ltd
LONDON EDINBURGH MELBOURNE AUCKLAND T(
HONG KONG SINGAPORE KUALA LUMPUR NEW
NAIROBI JOHANNESBURG LUSAKA IBADAN
KINGSTON

ISBN 0 435 23722 5

First published 1798

First published Hereford Plays 1977

Reprinted 1977

Published by
Heinemann Educational Books Ltd
48 Charles Street, London W1X 8AH
Set in 10/11pt Garamond by
Spectrum Typesetting, London
and printed in Great Britain by
Biddles Ltd, Guildford, Surrey

Contents

INTRODUCTION

by

Clifford Williams

It has been customary to regard the eighteenth and nineteenth centuries as a dead patch in the history of British drama. After the vivacity of the Restoration theatre one charts one's way through nearly two hundred years by reference to a handful of names—Nicholas Rowe, Richard Steele, Oliver Goldsmith, Richard Brinsley Sheridan, Dion Boucicault, Thomas William Robertson, Henry Arthur Jones, Arthur Wing Pinero, Oscar Wilde and George Bernard Shaw. Apart from these writers (and only some of them) few dramatists of the period are known or played. There were dozens of other writers producing plays, burlettas, operas and pantomimes at the time, but they rest in oblivion. John O'Keeffe was nearly one such.

I had never heard of O'Keeffe when I read *Wild Oats* in the autumn of 1976. Some months earlier the Literary Editor of the Royal Shakespeare Company, Ronald Bryden, had come across the play while making one of his frequent perambulations through the by-ways of English dramaturgy. The play had been put aside but a sudden gap in the RSC's programme at the Aldwych Theatre, its London home, brought it to notice again. I read it with some difficulty. The copy we had was a 19th century pamphlet type edition in miniscule typeface, and the diction and style of the piece was something of which I had little experience. I learnt from the preface to the play that O'Keeffe was nearly blind when he wrote it, and that he had written over seventy theatre plays and entertainments. I looked up O'Keeffe's brief entry in the *Oxford Companion to the Theatre* and found that the critic Hazlitt had described him as 'an English Molière'. (O'Keeffe was, in fact, Irish!)

When I had finished reading the play, I felt pleased by its

originality and good humour, and touched by the author's evident understanding of and affection for the theatre and all who worked in it. All the same, I went into rehearsal with some trepidation. I was aware that the actors were as charmed by the piece as I was, but had a healthy suspicion as to the stage-worthiness of a play which had remained on the shelf for so long. Ralph Koltai had designed the scenery, and we showed the company the model for the set. We had decided against using the sort of scenery which would have been employed for its original 18th century presentation. Instead, we opted for a simple but—hopefully—atmospheric setting. The play ranges through nine locales in the course of thirteen scenes. I had discovered that some nineteenth-century productions of it had lasted over four hours, and I could imagine that much of the time had passed in changing the scenery. We sought to avoid that situation by surrounding our stage with three walls constructed of simple planking which would remain as the surround for all the scenes. The walls were painted in bands of white, green and blue which gave something of an English landscape feeling though in an abstract fashion. Around the top of the walls ran a moulding which was also painted to blend with the walls. This moulding allowed our 'box' to be accepted as an *interior* when that was demanded by the action. Exits and entrances were made through swing doors let into the walls, but the doors were only noticeable when in use for they were otherwise flush with the walls and part of the overall painted 'environment'. We were also able to open slots in the side walls so as to slide through small flats which provided a background for certain scenes such as the interior of the *Sun Inn* and Bank's cottage, and we also 'flew' in various small scenic elements, for instance, a chandelier for Lady Amaranth's parlour. The furniture was restricted to a minimum—a table and two chairs for Amaranth, a bench for outside the *Sun,* the table and chair specifically described in the text for Banks, and so on. The furniture was set and struck between scenes by actors dressed as Quaker servants, inn servants, as appropriate, and to a musical accompaniment by Marc Wilkinson.

The costumes, designed by Judith Bland, were closely based on the style of the 1790s, with reference not only to the particular materials, cut and shape but also to the more intangible feeling of the age as evinced in the work of artists such as Thomas Rowlandson. The Quaker household were dressed strictly as Quakers. Sir George was costumed in full naval uniform, odd perhaps for a retired officer but essential for the scene where Rover believes Sir George to be an actor in the costume of a sea officer. Dory was likewise unmistakably a bo'sun. Ascertaining information on naval dress (for we had also to costume the 'deserters') proved unexpectedly tricky for we discovered through the Greenwich Maritime Museum and a deal of reading in naval literature that there was little standardisation of dress, especially for the lower ranks, until the mid nineteenth century. However, one of the joys of dealing with a 'period' play is the amount of material which one picks up on all manner of curious subjects! I knew rather more about the history of the British Navy, Quaker beliefs and conduct, 18th century legal practice, the laws of inheritance, the operation of turnpikes and revolutionary clergyman ('Parson Palmer') after directing *Wild Oats* than I had known before.

Our biggest piece of detective work was on the source of the many quotations spoken by Rover. Between themselves the actors soon cracked most of the Shakespearean quotes though once or twice Alan Howard, who was playing Rover, initially attributed lines from roles he had played to the wrong play (which he had also been in!). And there was a deal of confusion as to who spoke what and to whom in the *As You Like It* snippets. I thought I knew this play backwards but made several errors. Many of the Shakespeare quotes were garbled, and we were unable to decide whether this was by intention, or because of O'Keeffe relying on his memory, or if in fact he was following some adapted texts of Shakespeare which were common in the 18th century. We had much more trouble with the quotations borrowed from other playwrights for these came often from works which are virtually unknown today. One or two textual references also bothered us a great deal, in particular Rover's mentioning that he will put on his *Ranger* costume to visit Amaranth. We were halfway through our rehearsals before discovering that Ranger was a character in Dr Hoadley's *The Suspicious Husband*. I managed to find a copy of this play and noted with some satisfaction that it was entirely apt, for Ranger occupied himself with amorous intrigue whilst remaining a gentleman! Not dissimilar to Rover.

Our curiosity was equally aroused by the enigma of O'Keeffe himself. Who was he? What did his contemporaries think of him? What were the theatre and the audiences like in the time he was writing? Where did his work fit into the general development of drama in the 18th century? We were able to build some picture of the man from his memoirs which he wrote near the end of his life. We learnt of his struggles to support his family on his earnings as a dramatist, of his successes and failures, of his ill health and blindness, and of his dogged industry and courage. His devotion to the theatre and to all who worked in it shines through every page of *Recollections* and, above all, his paramount love for Shakespeare (*As You Like It* was his favourite play). We saw O'Keeffe bustling from play to play, trying to please managers, actors and audiences alike, meeting deadlines, constantly short of money yet ever generous, a vivacious practitioner of *boulevard* theatre but always alive to creative innovation and contemptuous of incompetent or untruthful writing and acting. Our growing respect for O'Keeffe was accompanied by our growing admiration for *Wild Oats*. Norman Rodway (Sir George), Joe Melia (Dory) and myself had many conversations about the sheer excellence of the structure of the play, the way in which O'Keeffe plotted entrances and exits, his managing of the story line, and his unfailing grasp of the balance to be struck between comedy and drama, humour and sentiment.

The basis of our approach to the production of the play was found however in an examination of the relationship between Rover and Amaranth. Rover, who does not know the secret of his own birth, goes in disguise to woo Amaranth who herself conceals a magical temperament beneath her austere Quaker outward show. A genuinely Shakespearean theme of concealed and mis-identities (compounded by the fact that nearly everyone else in the play is either actually or spiritually 'disguised')! But Rover also exists in a deeper form of disguise in that his conversation—for all its fluency—is largely that of other men or, rather, 'characters'. How was Rover viewed in the late 18th century? Did audiences of the time find him merely quaint and droll? Did they see in the play only O'Keeffe's expertise in cobbling together quotations? And was it O'Keeffe's sole intention to display the breadth of his knowledge of English drama through his use of quotation. The answer lies early in the play when Harry Thunder tells us before Rover enters—'In this forlorn stroller I discovered qualities that honour human nature, and accomplishments that might grace a prince'. Harry's opinion is confirmed by Amaranth—'A profane stage-player with such a gentle, generous heart! Yet so whimsically wild, like the unconscious rose, modestly shrinking from the recollection of its own grace and sweetness.' Rover is a man to be treated seriously.

Rover is 'forlorn' not only because he lacks means and recognition. More importantly, he lacks parents and identity. His high spirits frequently give place to moments of melancholy and anger, (even rage when he sees other 'forlorn' souls being put upon). He is a hero in search of his true inheritance, and until he can find that, not even his speech can be called his own. In the hands of a Strindberg or Pirandello such a hero might well have proved deranged and demented. But O'Keeffe's view of life, whatever the troubles in his own, is unfailingly optimistic and his purpose is compassionate and reconciliatory. In the last scene of the play, Rover discovers his parents, his identity, his inheritance, his 'unexpected blessings' and, ever devoted to his Muse of Fire, celebrates with a performance of *As You Like It*. Contemporary reports of theatre audiences in O'Keeffe's time leave us in no doubt that dissatisfaction with a play or an opera was expressed loudly and vociferously. But I am convinced that those same audiences who knew how to use their ears and were alive to rich and expressive speech (in a way denied to later ages fed on the pap of mass media) would have delighted in the warm conviction of *Wild Oats* that love of poetry and of man must eventually merit reward.

Whether O'Keeffe's audiences could enjoy the play more than we today because of a more intimate knowledge of the quotations employed is debatable. They saw more of the Restoration and Heroic plays quoted than we do, but some phrases are lifted from sources which must have been as obscure to them as to us. Early on in the RSC rehearsals I talked to Alan Howard about the way in which he would play the quotations. We agreed that there was not much point in presenting Rover as a *bad* actor of his day. All the internal evidence of *Wild Oats* and the general temper of the play suggests the opposite. We knew that the 18th century was well aware of the excesses of declamatory and exaggerated acting, and actors were striving for a more naturalistic style (though not helped in this aim by most of their dramatic confrères). We knew also that Rover normally played comedic roles and one would expect comic actors to be lighter in touch—on the whole—than tragedians. Alan Howard felt that the best plan would be to try and allow each quotation to emerge as naturally and organically as the moment or scene permitted. In this way, some quotations which were simple and unremarkable would pass by without requiring or affording notice. Some would be helped by flavouring them with a touch of that declamatory tone which Rover himself would probably eschew as an actor. An example of this would be 'I say my sister's wronged . . . Say that, Chamont' (Act II,ii) addressed to Sim. Sim is clearly meant to be impressed mightily by this heroic rhetorical utterance hence his comic rejoinder—'I think it's full moon'. He thinks Rover is mad not only because of what he has said but the way in which he has said it. A few lines later Rover is quoting Touchstone from *As You Like It* in conversation with Sim, but the rhythm of the scene is quick and light, and Rover must feather through these better known phrases. Still later Rover says with 'great feeling' (O'Keeffe's stage direction), quoting Gloucester from *Lear*—' 'Tho love cool, friendship fall off, brothers divide, subjects rebel, oh! never let the sacred bond be cracked 'twixt son and father!' Some actors might have over-emoted this speech during an actual 18th century production of *Lear,* but obviously Rover is meant to speak wth simplicity and sincerity for the gentle Sim's immediate response is unequivocal—'Ecod! he's not acting now!'

So bit by bit Alan Howard and I examined each quoted phrase in the light of Rover's character and the reason and situation which informed their usage. I was nevertheless fairly insistent during rehearsals (perhaps boringly so) that he should have at the back of his mind an *awareness* of when he was quoting which would lead to slight vocal 'italicising' of the quotations so that none should pass by without my being aware that they were there. But as he assimilated the role, I noticed that his Rover was taking a more spontaneous (and correct) course; that is, that Rover sometimes spoke in quotation without being aware of it, and that sometimes Rover consciously used an apt quotation which he selected to fit a given moment.

In performance we saw to our pleasure that modern audiences found no problem in the quotations whether known or otherwise. In practice, the better known phrases generally occur during comic scenes—''Tis I, Hamlet the Dane', 'Aye; to a nunnery go, go', etc, and these accentuate the humour (though O'Keeffe cunningly provides a situation which will work whether the phrases are recognized or not). Conversely, many of the lesser known quotations happen during moments when the romantic or poignant mood is strong enough to affect the audience even if they do not identify or are unaware of the quotation.

Producers and general readers of *Wild Oats* will have their own ideas about the characters and interpretation of the play. But there are some basic points about the staging of the play which should be considered.

1) Scenes should be allowed to follow on with rapidity (as with Shakespeare). This implies an unfussy and quickly changeable form of scenery and furniture.

2) Although there is some suggestion of a considerable passage of time within the play (for instance, Harry returns to naval school and then leaves again to seek his father) it is better to assume that it happens during the course of a single day. In the early morning, Sir George encounters his niece Lady Amaranth, and Rover and Harry part. Mid-morning Rover and Amaranth meet. Mid-day Rover finds himself at the *Sun Inn.* In the early afternoon most of the principal characters meet at Amaranth's and Sir George is taken for Mr Abrawang. In the late afternoon, Rover rescues Sir George from the ruffians. In the evening the dénouement takes place at Amaranth's and *As You Like It* is staged.

3) O'Keeffe's compact and idiosyncratic language makes *Wild Oats* perhaps a better play to read aloud or to act than to read to

oneself. His speech rhythms and idiom may be initially troublesome, but actors must learn to render them accurately. Once this is done the play's inner flow asserts itself. The key to performance lies in precise attention to the text, noting the Quaker phraseology, the nautical parlance, the country diction, the play quotations and the overall verbal liveliness with the employment of frequent alliteration, assonance and word-play.

The text must be played lightly and quickly, and this entails quick thinking and economical effort. But the watchword must be—as Harry says of Rover—'Hurried on by the impetuous flow of his own volatile spirits'.

4) The *aside* is used a great deal. Modern actors tend to distrust this convention and to throw away their asides, that is, to speak softly and quickly as if they were not there. The reverse method should be tried. Asides do not have to be bellowed but they are intended for the audience to hear and must be spoken firmly and clearly. When a character speaks an aside during the course of a conversation with another the latter should hold his ground, as it were, during the aside. He need not look away or at the ground or scratch his head, or invent some business to cover the period of the aside. The convention is that the aside simply does not exist for him—it is a suspended moment in the action, that is all. Audiences will accept and appreciate the convention providing the actors are not embarrassed by it.

5) The play is a comedy, but it is a comedy set in a time of much violence, poverty and injustice. Actors could be persecuted as rogues and vagabonds, poor men arbitrarily evicted. Life in the country was hard and gruelling. For all its wit and exuberance, *Wild Oats* reflects a genuine concern with the realities of late 18th century life. O'Keeffe has assembled a collection of eccentrics caught up in a 'rapid stream of extravagant whim', but his purpose is fundamentally serious—he proposes nothing short of the triumph of humanity and love in an often squalid, unsympathetic and perplexing world.

6) If the play is presented with one interval—then this is probably best placed at the end of Act III.

7) Twitch and the Sheriff's Officer may be played by one actor and as one character.

CHARACTERS

Sir George Thunder
Rover
Harry
Banks
John Dory
Farmer Gammon
Lamp
Ephraim Smooth
Sim
Zachariah
Muz
Trap
Twitch
Waiter
Landlord
Sheriff's Officer
1st Ruffian
2nd Ruffian
3rd Ruffian
Lady Amaranth
Amelia
Jane

Scene: Hampshire

CAST LIST OF THE ROYAL SHAKESPEARE COMPANY'S PRODUCTION

The Royal Shakespeare Company's production opened at the Aldwych Theatre on 14 December, 1976. The text used was that published by O'Keeffe in 1798, but some small deletions were made along the lines suggested in the 1805 edition. The cast was (in order of speaking):

John Dory	Joe Melia
Sir George Thunder	Norman Rodway
Ephraim Smooth	Patrick Godfrey
Lady Amaranth	Lisa Harrow
Zachariah	Simon Jones
Midge (Muz)	Doyne Byrd
Harry Thunder	Jeremy Irons
Rover	Alan Howard
Farmer Gammon	Raymond Westwell
Sim	Tim Wylton
Jane	Zoe Wanamaker
Banks	John Bott
Twitch	Tim Barlow
Waiters	Bille Brown
	James Cormack
Landlord	Raymond Marlowe
Trap	Joe Dunlop
Lamp	Richard Simpson
Maids	Emma Williams
	Diana Rowan
Amelia	Eve Pearce
First Ruffian	Bille Brown
Second Ruffian	Ben Cross
Third Ruffian	Doyne Byrd

MUSICIANS Jeremy Barlow, flute; Michael Lewin, guitar; Richard McLaughlin, harpsichord; Tony McVey, percussion; Kathleen Malet, violin; Peter Whittaker, bassoon.

Directed by   **Clifford Williams**

Designed by	Ralph Koltai
Costumes by	Judith Bland
Music by	Marc Wilkinson
Lighting by	Robert Ornbo
Assistant to Director	Amanda Knott
Stage Manager	Maggie Whitlum
Deputy Stage Manager	Titus Grant
Assistant Stage Manager	Caroline Howard
Sound	Roland Morrow

ACT ONE

SCENE ONE

A Parlour in **Lady Amaranth**'s.
Enter **John Dory**.

John: Fine cruizing this! without flip or biscuit! don't know who's the governor of this here fort; but if he can victual us a few—how hollow my bread-room sounds! (*striking his sides*) I'm as empty as a stoved keg, and as tired as an old Dutchman—my obstinate master, Sir George, to tow my old hulk—aboard the house, ha, hoy!

Sir George (*without*): John! John Dory!

John (*sits*): I'm at anchor.

    Enter **Sir George Thunder**.

Sir George: I don't know whose house we've got into here, John; but I think, when he knows me, we may hope for some refreshment—Eh! (*Looking at* **John**) Was not I your captain?

John: Yes, and I was your boatswain. And what of all that?

Sir George: Then how dare you sit in my presence, you bluff head?

John: Why, for the matter of that I don't mind; but had I been your captain, and you my boatswain, the man that stood by me at sea, should be welcome to sit before me at land. (*rising*)

Sir George: That's true, my dear John; offer to stand up, and, damme, if I don't knock you down—zounds! I am as dry as a powder match—to sail at the rate of ten knots an hour, over fallow and stubble, from my own house, half a league this side of Gosport, and not catch these deserters!

John: In this here chase, you wanted the ballast of wisdom.

Sir George: How, sirrah! hasn't my dear old friend, Dick

Broadside, got the command of the ship I so often fought myself—to man it for him with expedition, didn't I offer two guineas over the King's bounty to every seaman that would enter on board her? Havn't these three scoundrels fingered the shot, then ran, and didn't I do right to run after them? Damn the money! I no more mind that than a piece of clinker; but 'twas the pride of my heart to see my beloved ship (the Eagle) well manned, when my old friend is the commander.

John: But since you've laid yourself up in ordinary, retired to live in quiet, on your own estate, and had done with all sea affairs—

Sir George: John, John, a man should forget his own convenience for his country's good—Tho' Broadside's letter said these fellows were lurking about this part of Hampshire, yet still it's all hide and seek.

John: Your ill luck.

Sir George: Mine, you swab?

John: Ay, you've money and gold; but grace and good fortune have shook hands with you these nineteen years, for that rogue's trick you play'd poor Miss Amelia, by deceiving her with a sham marriage, when you passed yourself for Captain Seymour, and then putting off to sea, leaving her to break her poor heart, and since marrying another lady.

Sir George: Wasn't I forc'd to it by my father?

John: Ay; because she had a great fortin, her death too was a judgment upon you.

Sir George: Why, you impudent dog-fish, upbraid me with running into false bay, when you were my pilot? Wasn't it you even brought me the mock clergyman that performed the sham marriage with Amelia?

John (*aside*): Yes, you thought so; but I took care to bring you a real clergyman.

Sir George: But is this a time or place for your lectures? At home, abroad, sea, or land, you will still badger me! mention my Wild Oats again and—you scoundrel, since the night my bed-curtains took fire, aboard the Eagle, you've got me quite into leading-strings—you snatched me upon deck, and tossed me into the sea,—to save me from being burnt. I was almost drowned.

John: You would but for me—

Sir George: Yes, you dragg'd me out by the ear like a water-dog—and 'cause applauded for that, ever since you're so curst careful of me, that only lifting my leg to step aboard a boat, you whip me up, and chuck me into it—last week, 'cause you found the tenth bottle uncorked, you rushed in among my friends and ran away with me, and, next morning Captain O'Shanaghan sends me a challenge for slinking off when he was toastmaster! so, to save me from a headache, you'd like to've got my brains blown out.

John: Oh, very well, be burnt in your bed, and tumble in the water by jumping into boats, like a tight fellow as you are, and poison yourself with sloe-juice; see if John cares a piece of mouldy biscuit about it. But I wish you hadn't made me your valet-de-Shamber. No sooner was I got on shore after five years dashing among rocks, shoals, and breakers, than you sets me on a high trotting cart-horse, which knock't me up and down like an old bomb-boat in the Bay of Biscay, and here's nothing to drink after all! because at home you keep open house, you think everybody else does the same.

Sir George: Why, by sailing into this strange port we may be more free than welcome.

John: Holloa! I'll never cease piping 'till it calls up a drop to wet my whistle. *(Exit)*

Sir George: Yes, as John Dory remarks, I fear my trip thro' life will be attended with heavy squalls and foul weather. When my conduct to poor Amelia comes athwart my mind, it's a hurricane for that day, and turn in at night, the ballad of 'William and Margaret' rings in my ear *(sings)* 'In glided Margaret's grimly ghost' oh, zounds! the dismals are coming upon me, and can't get a cheering glass to—holloa!

    Enter **Ephraim Smooth**.

Ephraim: Friend, what woulds't thou have?

Sir George: Grog.

Ephraim: Neither man nor woman of that name abideth here.

Sir George: Ha, ha, ha! man and woman! then if you'll bring me Mr Brandy and Mrs Water, we'll couple them, and the first child will probably be master Grog.

Ephraim: Thou dost speak in parables, which I understand not.

Sir George: Sheer off with your sanctified poop, and send the gentleman of the house.

Ephraim: The owner of this mansion is a maiden, and she approacheth.

    Enter **Lady Amaranth.**

Lady Amaranth: Friend, Ephraim Smooth, did'st thou— *(turns, sees* **Sir George***)* do I behold? It is! how dost thou, uncle?

Sir George: Is it possible you can be my niece, Lady Maria Amaranth Thunder?

Lady Amaranth: I am the daughter of thy deceased brother Loftus, called Earl Thunder, but no Lady, my name is Mary.

Sir George: But, how is all this? Eh! unexpectedly find you in a strange house, of which old Sly here tells me you're mistress, turned Quaker and disclaim your title!

Lady Amaranth: Title is vanity.

Sir George: Why certainly I drop my Lord by courtesy for my Sir Knighthood acquired by my own merit girl.

Lady Amaranth: Thou knowest the relation to whose care my father left me?

Sir George: Well! I know our cousin, old Dovehouse, was a Quaker! but I didn't suspect he would have made you one.

Lady Amaranth: Being now gathered to his fathers, he did bequeath unto me his worldly goods; amongst them, this mansion and the lands around it.

Ephraim: So thou becom'st and continue one of the faithful. I am executor of his will, and by it, I cannot give thee, Mary, possession of these goods but on those conditions.

Sir George: Tell me of your thee's and thou's, Quaker's wills and mansions! I say girl, tho' on the death of your father, my eldest brother, Loftus, Earl Thunder, from your being a female, his title devolved to his next brother, Robert; tho' as a woman, you can't be an Earl, nor as a woman you can't make laws for your sex and our sex, yet as the daughter of a Peer, you are, and, by heaven, shall be called Lady Maria Amaranth Thunder.

Ephraim: Thou makest too much noise, friend.

Sir George: Call me friend and I'll bump your block against the capstern.

Ephraim: Yea, this is a man of danger, and I'll leave Mary to abide it. *(Exit)*

Sir George: 'Sfire, my Lady—

Enter Zachariah.

Zachariah: Shall thy cook, this day, roast certain birds of the air, called woodcocks, and ribs of the oxen likewise?

Lady Amaranth: All. My uncle sojourneth with me peradventure, and my meal shall be a feast, friend Zachariah.

Zachariah: My tongue shall say so, friend Mary.

Sir George: Sir George Thunder bids thee remember to call your mistress, Lady Amaranth.

Zachariah: Verily, George.

Sir George: George! sirrah, tho' a younger brother, the honour of knighthood was my reward for placing the British flag over that of a daring enemy—therefore address me with respect.

Zachariah: Yea, I do, good George. *(Exit)*

Sir George: George and Mary! here's levelling, here's abolition of title with a vengeance! in this house, they think no more of an English knight than a French Duke.

Lady Amaranth: Kinsman, be patient, thou, and thy son, my cousin Henry, whom I have not beheld I think, these twelve years, shall be welcome to my dwelling. Where now abideth the youth?

Sir George: At the Naval Academy, at Portsmouth.

Lady Amaranth: May I not see the young man?

Sir George: What, to make a Quaker of him?—No, no. *(aside)* But, hold, as she's now a wealthy heiress, her marrying my son Harry, will keep up and preserve her title in our own family too. Would'st thou really be glad to see him? thou shalt, Mary. Ha, ha, ha! John Dory, *(calling)* here comes my Valet de Chambre.

Enter John Dory.

John: Why, Sir—such a breeze sprung up?

Sir George: Avast, old man of war; you must instantly convoy my son from Portsmouth.

John: Then I must first convoy him to Portsmouth, for he happens to be out of dock already.

Sir George: What wind now?

John: You know on our quitting harbour—

Sir George: Damn your sea-jaw, you marvellous dolphin, give the contents of your log-book in plain English.

John: The young squire has cut and run.

Sir George: What!

John: Got leave to come to you, and master didn't find out before yesterday, that, instead of making for home, he had sheer'd off towards London, directly sent notice to you, and Sam has traced us all the way here to bring you the news.

Sir George: What, a boy of mine quits his guns? I'll grapple him.—Come John, come along.

Lady Amaranth: Order the carriage for mine uncle.

Sir George: No, thank ye, my Lady. Let your equipage keep up your own dignity. I've horses here; but I won't knock 'em up; next village is the channel for the stage—My Lady, I'll bring the dog to you by the bowsprit.—Weigh anchor! crowd sail! and after him! *(Exeunt)*

> *Re-enter* **Ephraim Smooth**, *peeping in.*

Ephraim: The man of noise doth not tarry, then my spirit is glad.

Lady Amaranth: Let Sarah prepare chambers for my kinsman, and hire the maiden for me that thou didst mention.

Ephraim: I will; for this damsel is passing fair, and hath found grace in mine eyes. Mary, as thou art yet a stranger in this land, and have just taken possession of this estate, the laws of society command thee to be on terms of amity with thy wealthy neighbours.

Lady Amaranth: Yea; but while I entertain the rich, the hearts of the poor shall also rejoice; I myself will now go forth into the adjacent hamlet, and invite all to hearty cheer.

Ephraim: Yea, I will distribute among the poor, the good books thou didst desire me.

Lady Amaranth: And meat and drink too, friend Ephraim. In the fullness of plenty they shall join in thanksgiving for those gifts which I overabundantly possess.

> *Exeunt.*

SCENE TWO

A road.
Enter **Harry Thunder,** *and* **Muz.**

Muz: I say Dick Buskin! harky, my lad!

Harry: What keeps Rover?

Muz: I'm sure I don't know. As you desired, I paid for our breakfast. But the devil's in that fellow, every Inn we stop at he will always hang behind, chattering to the bar-maid, or chambermaid.

Harry: Or any, or no maid. But he's a worthy lad. And I love him better, I think, than my own brother, had I one.

Muz: Oh! but, Dick, mind, my boy—

Harry: Stop, Muz. Tho' twas my orders when I set out on this scamper with the players, (the better to conceal my quality,) for you, before people, to treat me as your companion; yet, at the same time, you should have had discretion enough to remember, when we're alone, that I am still your master, and son to Sir George Thunder.

Muz: Sir, I ask your pardon; but by making yourself my equal, I've got so used to familiarity, that I find it hard to shake it off.

Harry: Well, Sir, pray mind, that familiarity is all over now. My frolic's out, I now throw off the player, and shall directly return. My father must by this time have heard of my departure from the academy at Portsmouth; and, tho' I was deluded away by my rage for a little acting, yet 'twas wrong of me to give the gay old fellow any cause for uneasiness.

Muz: And, Sir, shall you and I never act another scene together?

Shall I never again play Colonel Standard for my own benefit? Never again have the pleasure of caning your honour in the character of Tom Errand.

Harry: In future act the part of a smart hat and coat brusher, or I shall have the honour of kicking you in the character of an idle puppy. You were a good servant; but I find, by letting you crack your jokes and sit in my company, you're grown quite a lounging rascal.

Muz: Yes, Sir, I was a modest, well behaved lad; but evil communication corrupts good manners.

Harry: Begone, Sir, 'till I call for you.

Exit **Muz**.

Well, if my father but forgives me.—This three months excursion has shown me some life, and a devilish deal of fun. For one circumstance, I shall ever remember it with delight. It's bringing me acquainted with Jack Rover. How long he stays! Jack! In this forlorn stroller I have discovered qualities that honour human nature, and accomplishments that might grace a Prince. I don't know a pleasanter fellow, except when he gets to his abominable habit of quotation. I hope he won't find the purse I've hid in his coat pocket, before we part. I dread the moment, but it's come.

Rover *(without)*: 'The brisk li-li-lightning I.'

Harry: Ay, here's the rattle. Hurried on by the impetuous flow of his own volatile spirits, his life is a rapid stream of extravagant whim, and while the serious voice of humanity prompts his heart to the best of actions, his features shine in laugh and levity. Studying Bayes, eh, Jack?

Enter **Rover**.

Rover: 'I am the bold Thunder.'

Harry *(aside)*: I am if he knew but all.—Keep one standing in the road.

Rover: Beg your pardon, my dear Dick! but all the fault of—Plague on't, that a man can't sleep and breakfast at an inn, then return up to his bedchamber for his gloves that he'd forgot; but there he must find chambermaids thumping feathers and knocking pillows about, and keep one when one has affairs and business! 'Pon my soul, these girls conduct to us is intolerable. The very thought brings the blood into my face, and whenever they attempt to serve, provoke me so, damme but I will, I will—An't I right, Dick?

Harry: 'No; all in the wrong.'

Rover: No matter, that's the universal play 'all around the wrekin': but you're so conceited, because by this company you're going to join at Winchester, you are engaged for high tragedy.

Harry: And you for Rangers, Plumes and Foppingtons.

Rover: Our first play is *Lear*. I was devilish imperfect in Edgar t'other night at Lymington. I must look it over. *(takes out a book)*, 'Away, the foul fiend follows me!' Hollo! stop a moment, we shall have the whole county after us. *(Going)*

Harry: What now?

Rover: That rosy-faced chambermaid put me in such a passion, that by heaven, I walked out of the house, and forgot to pay our bill. *(Going)*

Harry: Never mind, Rover, it's paid.

Rover: Paid! Why, neither you nor Muz had money enough. No, really!

Harry: Ha, ha, ha! I tell you, it is.

Rover: You paid? Oh, very well. Every honest fellow should be a stock purse. Come then, let's push on now. Ten miles to Winchester, we shall be there by eleven.

Harry: Our trucks are booked at the inn for the Winchester coach.

Rover: 'Ay, to foreign climates my old trunk I bear.' But I prefer walking, to the Car of Thespis.

Harry: Which is the way?

Rover: Here.

Harry *(pointing opposite)*: Then I go there.

Rover: Eh!

Harry: My dear boy, on this spot, and at this moment, we must part.

Rover: Part!

Harry: Rover, you wish me well.

Rover: Well, and suppose so. Part, eh! What mystery and grand? What are you at? Do you forget, you, Muz, and I are engaged to Truncheon, the manager, and that the bills are already up with our names to-night to play at Winchester?

Harry: Jack, you and I have often met on a stage in assumed characters; if it's your wish we should ever meet again in our real ones, of sincere friends, without asking whither I go, or my motives for leaving you, when I walk up this road, do you turn down that.

Rover: Joke!

Harry: I'm serious. Good'bye!

Rover: If you repent your engagement with Truncheon, I'll break off too, and go with you wherever you will—*(takes him under the arm)*.

Harry: Attempt to follow me, and even our acquaintance ends.

Rover: Eh!

Harry: Don't think of my reasons, only that it must be.

Rover: Have I done anything to—Dick Buskin leave me! *(turns and puts his handkerchief to his eyes)*

Harry: I am as much concern'd as you—Good'bye.

Rover: I can't even bid him good'bye—I won't neither—If any cause could have given—Farewell.

Harry: Bless my poor fellow! Adieu. *(silently weeps)*
   Exeunt severally.

END OF THE FIRST ACT

ACT TWO

SCENE ONE

A Village; a Farm House, and near it a Cottage.
Enter **Farmer Gammon**, and **Ephraim Smooth**.

F. Gammon: Well, Master Ephraim, I may depend on thee, as you Quakers never break your words.

Ephraim: I have spoken to Mary, and she, at my request, consenteth to take thy daughter, Jane, as her handmaid.

F. Gammon: Very good of you.

Ephraim *(aside)*: Goodness I do like, and also—comely Jane. The maiden, I will prefer for the sake of—myself.

F. Gammon: I intended to make a present to the person that did me such a piece of service; but I sha'nt affront you with it.

Ephraim: I am meek and humble, and must take affronts.

F. Gammon: Then here's a guinea, master Ephraim.

Ephraim: I expected not this; but there is no harm in a guinea. *(Exit)*

F. Gammon: So I shall get my children off my hands.—My son, Sim, robbing me day and night—giving away my corn and what not among the poor; and daughter Jane, to prevent me from killing the fowls, buys eggs, and tells me they are still laying them; besides, when girls have nought to do, this love-mischief creeps into their heads.—*(calling)* Sim!
Enter **Sim**.

Sim: Yes, feyther.

F. Gammon: Call your sister.

Sim: Jane, feyther wants you.
Enter **Jane**, *from the House*.

Jane: Did you call me?

11

F. Gammon: I often told you both, but it's now settled; you must go out into the world and work for your bread.

Sim: Well, feyther, whatever you think right, must be so, and I'm content.

Jane: And I'm sure, feyther, I'm willing to do as you'd have me.

F. Gammon: There's ingratitude! When my wife died, I brought you both up from the shell, and now you want to fly off and forsake me.

Sim: Why, no; I'm willing to live with you all my days.

Jane: And I'm sure, feyther, if it's your desire, I'll never part from you.

F. Gammon: What, you want to hang upon me like a couple of leeches, ay, to strip my branches, and leave me with a withered hawthorn! See who's yon.

   Exit **Sim**.

Jane, Ephraim Smooth has hired you for Lady Amaranth.

Jane: O Lack! Then I shall live in the great house.

F. Gammon: Ay, and mayhap come in for her cast off clothes.

Jane: But she's a Quaker; and I'm sure, every Sunday for church, I dress much finer than her ladyship.

F. Gammon *(opens a book)*: She has sent us all presents of good books, to read a chapter in now and then. 'The Economy of Human Life.' Ah, I like Economy—read that—when a man's in a passion, this may give him patience; there Jane. *(gives her the book)*

Jane: Thank her good ladyship.

F. Gammon: My being encumber'd with you both is the cause why old Banks won't give me his sister.

Jane: That's a pity. If we must have a step-mother, Madam Amelia would make us a very good one. But I wonder how she can refuse you, feyther, for I'm sure she must think you a very portly man in your scarlet vest and new scratch. You can't think how parsonable you'd look, if you'd only shave twice a week, and put sixpence in the poor-box on a Sunday. *(Retires reading)*

F. Gammon: However, if Banks still refuses, I have him in my power. I'll turn them both out of their cottage yonder, and the bailiff shall provide them with a lodging.

   Enter **Banks**.

Well, neighbour Banks, once for all, am I to marry your sister?

Banks: That she best knows.

F. Gammon: Ay, but she says she won't.

Banks: Then I dare say she won't; for I never knew her to speak what she didn't think.

F. Gammon: Then she won't have me? A fine thing this, that you and she, who are little better than paupers, dare be so saucy!

Banks: Why, farmer, I confess we're poor: but while that's the worst our enemies can say of us, we're content.

F. Gammon: Od, dom it! I wish I had now a good, fair occasion to quarrel with him; I'd make him content with a devil; I'd knock 'en down, send him to jail and—But I'll be up with him!

Enter **Sim**.

Sim: Oh, feyther, here's one Mr Lamp, a ringleader of Showfolks come from Andover to act in our village. He wants a barn to play in, if you'll hire him yourn.

F. Gammon: Surely, boy. I'll never refuse money. But, lest he should engage the great room in the inn, run thou and tell him—Stop, I'll go myself—A short cut through that garden *(going thro' the Cottage garden,* **Banks** *stops him)*.

Banks: Why, you, or any neighbour is welcome to walk in it, or to partake of what it produces, but making it a common thoroughfare is—

F. Gammon: Here, Sim, kick open that garden gate.

Banks: What?

F. Gammon: Does the lad hear?

Sim: Why, yes, yes.

F. Gammon: Does the fool understand?

Sim: I'm as yet but young; but if understanding teaches me how to wrong my neighbour, may I never live to years of discretion.

F. Gammon: What, you cur, do you disobey your feyther? Burst open the garden gate, as I command you.

Sim: Feyther, he that made both you and the garden, commands me not injure the unfortunate.

F. Gammon: Here's an ungracious rogue! Then I must do it myself. *(Advances)*

Banks *(stands before it)*: Hold, neighbour. Small as this spot is, it's now my only possession: and the man shall first take my life who sets a foot in it against my will.

F. Gammon: I'm in such a passion.—

Jane *(comes forward)*: Feyther, if you're in a passion, read the 'Economy of Human Life'. *(offers book)*

F. Gammon: Plague of the wench! But, you hussy, I'll—and you, you unlucky bird!

 Exeunt **Sim** *and* **Jane**.

 Shower of Rain. Enter **Rover** *hastily.*

Rover: Here's a pelting shower and no shelter! 'Poor Tom's a cold.' I'm wet thro'. Oh, here's a fair promising house. *(going to* **Gammon***'s)*

F. Gammon *(stops him)*: Hold, my lad. Can't let folks in till I know who they be. There's a public house not above a mile on.

Banks: Step in here, young man; My fire is small; but it shall cheer you with a hearty welcome.

Rover *(to* **Banks***)*: The poor cottager! *(to* **Gammon***)* And the substantial farmer! *(kneels)* 'Hear, Nature, dear goddess, hear! If ever you designed to make his cornfields fruitful, change thy purpose; that, from the blighted ear no grain may fall to fat his stubble goose—and, when to town he drives his hogs, so like himself, oh, let him feel the soaking rain, then may he curse his crime too late, and know how sharper than a serpent's tooth it is.'—Damme, but I'm spouting in the rain all this time.

 Rises and runs into **Bank***'s cottage.*

F. Gammon: Ay, neighbour, you'll soon rise from a beggar's bed if you harbour every mad vagrant. This may be one of the footpads, that, it seems, have got about the country; but I'll have an execution, and seize on thy goods, this day, my charitable neighbour! Eh, the sun strikes out, quite cleared up.

 Enter **Jane**.

Jane: La, feyther, if there isn't coming down the village—

F. Gammon: Ah, thou hussy!

Jane: Bless me, feyther! No time for anger now. Here's Lady

Amaranth's chariot, drawn by her new grand long tail'd horses.—La! it stops!

F. Gammon: Her Ladyship is coming out, and walks this way.—She may wish to rest herself in my house. Jane, we must always make rich folks welcome.

Jane: Dear me, I'll run in and set things to rights. But, feyther, your cravat and wig are all got so rumplified with your cross grain'd tantarums.—I'll tie your neck-cloth in a big bow, and for your wig, if there is any flour in the drudging-box—*(adjusts them and runs into house)*.

F. Gammon: Oh! the bailiff too that I engaged.—

Enter **Twitch**.

Twitch: Well, Master Gammon, as you desired, I'm come to serve this here warrant of yours, and arrest master Banks; where is he?

F. Gammon: Yes, now I be's determined on't—he's—Stand aside, I'll speak to you anon. *(looking out)*

Enter **Lady Amaranth**, **Zachariah** *following*.

Lady Amaranth: Friend, Jane, whom I have taken to be my handmaid, is thy daughter?

F. Gammon: Ay so her mother said, an't please your Ladyship.

Lady Amaranth: Ephraim Smooth acquainteth me thou art a wealthy yeoman.

F. Gammon: Why, my Lady, I pay my rent.

Lady Amaranth: Being yet a stranger on my estate around here, I have passed through thy hamlet to behold with mine own eye, the distresses of my poor tenants. I wish to relieve their wants.

F. Gammon: Right, your Ladyship: for charity hides a deal of sins. How good of you to think of the poor! that's so like me. I'm always contriving how to relieve my neighbours—*(apart to* **Twitch***)* You must lay Banks in jail tonight.

Enter **Jane**.

Jane: A'nt please you, will your ladyship enter our humble dwelling and rest your ladyship in feyther's great cane-bottom'd elbow chair with a high back. *(curtsies)*

F. Gammon: Do, my Lady. To receive so great a body from her own chariot is an honour I dreamt not of; tho' for the hungry and weary foot traveller, my doors are always open and my

15

morsel ready. *(apart to* **Twitch***)* Knock; when he comes out, touch him.

Lady Amaranth: Thou art benevolent, and I will enter thy dwelling with satisfaction.

Jane: O precious! This way, my lady.

Exeunt all but **Twitch**.

Twitch: Eh, where's the warrant? *(feels his pocket, and knocks at* **Bank's** *door)*.

Enter **Banks**.

Banks: Master Twitch! What's your business with me?

Twitch: Only a little affair here against you.

Banks: Me!

Twitch: Yes; farmer Gammon has bought up a thirty pound note of hand of yours.

Banks: Indeed! I didn't think this malice could have stretched so far—I thought the love he professed for my sister, might—why, it's true, master Twitch, to lend our indigent cottagers small sums when they've been unable to pay their rents, I got lawyer Quirk to procure me this money, and hoped their industry would have put it in my power to take up my note before now. However, I'll go round and try what they can do, then call on you and settle it.

Twitch: No, no, you must go with me.

Rover *(without)*: Old gentleman come quick, or I'll open another bottle of your currant wine.

Twitch *(to* **Banks***)*: You'd best not make a noise, but come.

Enter **Rover**.

Rover: Oh, you're here? Rain over—quite fine—I'll take a sniff of the open air too—Eh, what's the matter?

Twitch: What's that to you?

Rover: What's that to me? Why, you're a very unmannerly—

Twitch: Oh, here's a rescue!

Banks: Nay, my dear Sir, I'd wish you not to bring yourself into trouble about me.

Twitch: Now, since you don't know what's civil, if the debt's not paid directly, to jail you go.

Rover: My kind, hospitable good old man to jail! What's the amount, you scoundrel.

Twitch: Better words, or I'll—

Rover: Stop; utter you a word good or bad, except to tell me what's your demand upon this gentleman, and I'll give you the greatest beating you ever got since the hour you commenced rascal. *(in a low tone)*

Twitch: Why, master, I don't want to quarrel with you, because—

Rover: You'll get nothing by it. Do you know, you villain, that I am this moment the greatest man living?

Twitch: Who, pray?

Rover: 'I am the bold Thunder!' Sirrah, know that I carry my purse of gold in my coat-pocket. *(aside and takes it out)*. Tho' damme if I know how a purse came there. There's twenty pictures of his Majesty; therefore, in the King's name, I free his liege subject, *(takes* **Banks** *away)* and now who am I? Ah, ah!

Twitch: Nine pieces short, my master; but if you're a housekeeper I'll take this and your bail.

Rover: Then for bail you must have a housekeeper? What's to be done?

    Enter **Gammon**.

Ah, here's little Hospitality! I know you've a house, tho' your fire-side was too warm for me. Lookye, here's some rapacious, griping rascal, has had this worthy gentleman arrested. Now a certain good for nothing, rattling fellow has paid twenty guineas of the debt, you pass your word for the other nine, we'll step back into the old gentleman's friendly house, and over his currant wine, our first toast shall be, liberty to the honest debtor, and confusion to the hard hearted creditor.

F. Gammon: Shan't.

Rover: Shan't! Pray an't your name Mr Shylock—

F. Gammon: No, my name's Gammon.

Rover: Gammon! You're the Hampshire hog.

    Exit **F. Gammon**.

S'death! How shall I do to extricate—?

    Enter **Lady Amaranth**, *from* **Gammon**'s.

Lady Amaranth: What tumult's this?

Rover: A lady! *(bows)* Ma'am, your most obedient humble servant. *(aside)* A quaker too! They are generally kind and humane, and that face is the prologue to a play of a thousand good acts—maybe she'd help us here. Ma'am, you must know that—that I—no—this gentleman—I mean this gentleman and I—He got a little behindhand, as any honest, well principled man often may, from bad harvests and rains—lodging corn—and his cattle—from murrain, and—rot and rot the murrain! You know this is the way all this affair happened *(to* **Banks***)* and then up steps this gentleman *(to* **Twitch***)* with a—a tip in his way—madam, you understand? And then in steps I—with my a—In short, madam, I am the worst story teller in the world where myself is the hero of the tale.

Twitch: In plain English, Mr Banks has been arrested for thirty pounds, and this gentleman has paid twenty guineas of the debt.

Banks: My litigious neighbour to expose me thus!

Lady Amaranth: The young man and maiden within, have spoken well of thy sister, and pictured thee as a man of irreproachable morals though unfortunate.

Rover: Madam, he's the honestest fellow—I've known him above forty years, he has the best hand at stirring a fire—If you were only to taste his currant wine.

Banks: Madam, I never aspired to an enviable rank in life: but hitherto pride and prudence kept me above the reach of pity: but obligations from a stranger—

Lady Amaranth: He really a stranger, and attempt to free thee? But friend *(to* **Rover***)* thou hast assumed a right which here belongeth alone to me. As I enjoy the blessings which these lands produce, I own also the heart delighting privilege of dispensing those blessings to the wretched. Thou mads't thyself my worldly banker, and no cash of mine in thine hands, *(takes a note from a pocket book)* but thus I balance our account. *(offers it)*

Rover: 'Madam, my master pays me, nor can I take money from another hand without injuring his honour and disobeying his commands.'

'Run, run, Orlando, carve on every tree
The fair, the chaste, the unexpressive she.'
Runs off.

Banks: But, sir, I insist you'll return him his money. *(to* **Twitch***)*

Stop! *(going)*

Twitch: Ay, stop! *(holds the skirt of his coat)*

Lady Amaranth: Where dwelleth he?

Banks: I fancy, where he can, Madam. I understand, from his discourse, that he was on his way to join a company of actors in the next town.

Lady Amaranth: A profane stage-player with such a gentle, generous heart! Yet, so whimsically wild, like the unconscious rose, modestly shrinking from the recollection of its own grace and sweetness.

Enter Jane, *from the house, dressed.*

Jane: Now, my lady, I'm fit to attend your ladyship. *(aside)* I look so genteelish mayhap her ladyship may take me home with her.

Lady Amaranth *(aside)*: This maiden may find out for me whither he goeth. *(to* **Twitch***)* Call on my steward, and thy legal demands shall be satisfied.

Jane *(calls off)*: Here, coachman, drive up my lady.'s chariot, nearer to our door. *(aside)* If she'd take me with her, la! how all the folks will stare. Madam, tho' the roads are so very dusty, I'll walk all the way on foot to your ladyship's house—ay, though I should spoil my bran new petticoat.

Lady Amaranth: Rather than sully thy garment, thou shalt be seated by me.

Jane: Oh, your ladyship! *(aside)* he, he, he! If I didn't think so—

Enter Sim.

Here you Sim, order the chariot for us.

Sim: Us! Come, come, Jane, I've the little tax cart to carry you.

Jane: Cart!

Lady Amaranth: Friend be cheerful; thine and thy sister's sorrows shall be but an April shower.

Exeunt severally.

SCENE TWO

Before an Inn.
Enter **Rover** *and* **Waiter**.

Rover: Hillo! friend, when does the coach set out for London?

Waiter: In about an hour, sir.

Rover: Has the Winchester coach passed yet?

Waiter: No, sir. *(Exit)*

Rover: That's lucky! Then my trunk is here still. Go I will not. Since I've lost the fellowship of my friend Dick, I'll travel no more. I'll try a London audience, who knows but I may get an engagement. This celestial lady quaker! She must be rich, and ridiculous for such a poor dog as I, even to think of her. How Dick would laugh at me if he knew—I dare say by this she has released my kind host from the gripe of that rascal—I should like to be certain tho'.

    Enter **Landlord**.

Landlord: You'll dine here sir? I'm honest Bob Johnstone; kept the Sun these twenty years. Excellent dinner on table at two.

Rover: 'Yet my love indeed is appetite, I'm as hungry as the sea, and can digest as much.'

Landlord: Then you won't do for my shilling ordinary, sir, there's a very good ordinary at the Saracen's Head, at the end of the town. Shouldn't have thought indeed, hungry foot travellers to eat like aldermen—Coming, sir.

Rover: I'll not join this company at Winchester. No, I'll not stay in the country hopeless even to expect a look, (except of scorn) from this lady. I will take a touch at a London theatre. The public there, are candid and generous, and before my merit can have time to create enemies, I'll have money, and,—'a fig for the sultan and sophy'.

Enter **Jane** *at the back, and* **Sim** *watching her.*

Jane: Ay, that's he!

Rover: But if I fall, by heaven, I'll overwhelm the manager, his empire, and—'himself in one prodigious ruin'.

Jane: Oh lord! *(runs back)*

Sim: What can you expect when you follow young men? I've dodged you all the way.

Jane: Well! wasn't I sent?

Sim: Oh yes, you were sent—very likely. Who sent you?

Jane: It was—*(aside)* I won't tell it's my lady, 'cause she bid me not.

Sim: I'll keep you from sheame—a fine life I should have in the parish, rare fleering, if a sister of moine should stand some Sunday at church, in a white sheet, and to all their flouts what could I say?

Rover: Thus, 'I say my sister's wronged, my sister Blowsabella, born as high and noble as the attorney—do her justice, or by the gods, I'll lay a scene of blood, shall make this haymow horrible to Beedles.'—'Say that, Chamont.'

Sim: I believe it's full moon. You go hoame to your place, and moind your business.

Jane: My lady will be so pleased I found him! I don't wonder at it, he's such a fine spoken man.

Sim: Dang it! Will you stand here grinning at the wild bucks. You saucy slut, to keep me and the cart there waiting for you at the end of the lane.

Jane: Never mind him, sir; it's because my lady gave me a ride in her coach that makes the boy so angry.

Rover: 'Then you are Kastrill, the angry boy?'

Sim: So was the prime minister till he got himself shaved.

Jane: Perhaps the gentleman might wish to send her ladyship a compliment. A'nt please you, sir, if it's even a kiss between us two, it shall go safe; for though you should give it me, brother Sim then can take it to my lady.

Rover: 'I'd kiss'd thee ere I kill'd thee.'

Jane: Kill me!

Rover: 'No way but this killing myself to die upon a kiss!'

21

(advancing)

Sim *(interposing)*: And you walk home, my forward miss. *(mimicks)*

Rover: 'I've heard of your painting too: you gig, you lisp, you amble, and nickname God's creatures.'

Sim: Why, who told you she call'd me an ass?

Rover: 'Oh that the town clerk was here, to write thee down an ass! but though not written down in black and white, remember, thou art an ass.'

Jane: Yes, sir; I'll remember it.

Sim: Go! *(to* **Jane**—*puts her out.)*

Rover: 'Aye, to a nunnery go.' I'm cursedly out of spirits; but hang sorrow, I may as well divert myself.—''Tis meat and drink for me to see a clown.' 'Shepherd, was't ever at court?'

Sim: Not I.

Rover: 'Then thou art damn'd.'

Sim: Eh!

Rover: Ay! 'like an ill-roasted egg—all on one side.'—Little Hospitality. *(looking out)*

    Enter **Farmer Gammon**.

F. Gammon: Eh, where's the showman that wants to hire my barn? So, madame Jane, I place her out to sarvice, and instead of attending her mistress, she gets galloping all about the village,—How's this, son?

Rover: 'Your son? Young Clodpate, take him to your wheat-stack, and there teach him manners.'

F. Gammon: Ah, thou'rt the fellow that would bolt out of the dirty roads into people's houses. Ho, ho, ho! Sim's schooling is mightily thrown away, if he hasn't more manners than thou.

Sim: Why, feyther, it is! Gadzooks, he be one of the play! Acted Tom Fool, in King Larry, at Lymington, t'other night—I thought I know'd the face, tho' he had a straw cap, and blanket about'n.—Ho, ho! how comical that was when you said—

Rover: 'Pillicock sat upon Pillicock hill, pil-i-loo, loo!'

Sim: That's it! That's it! He's at it! *(claps)* Laugh, feyther, laugh.

F. Gammon: Hold your tongue, boy! I believe he's no better than he should be. The moment I saw him, says I to myself, you are a rogue.

Rover: There you spoke truth for once in your life.

F. Gammon: I'm glad to hear you confess it. But her ladyship shall have the vagrants whippt out of the country.

Rover: Vagrant! 'Thou wretch! despite o'erwhelm thee!' 'Only squint, and by heaven, I'll beat thy blown body 'till it rebounds like a tennis ball.'

Sim: Beat my feyther! No, no. Thou must first beat me. *(puts himself in a posture of defence)*

Rover *(with feeling)*: 'Tho' love cool, friendship fall off, brothers divide, subjects rebel, oh! never let the sacred bond be crackt 'twixt son and father!'—I never knew a father's protection, never had a father to protect. *(puts his handkerchief to his eyes)*

Sim: Ecod! he's not acting now!

Enter **Landlord**, *with a Book, Pen and Ink.*

F. Gammon: Landlord, is this Mr Lamp here?

Landlord: I've just opened a bottle for him and the other gentleman in the parlour.

Rover: 'Go, father, with thy son give him a livery more guarded than his fellows.'

Sim: Livery! Why, I be no sarvant man, tho' sister Jane is. Gi's thy hand. *(to* **Rover***)* I don't know how 'tis, but I think I could lose my life for thee; but mustn't let feyther be beat tho'—No, no! *(going, turns and looks at* **Rover***)* Ecod, I never shall forget Pillicock upon a hill!

Exeunt **Farmer Gammon**, *and* **Sim**.

Rover: 'Thou art an honest reptile'; I'll make my entrée on the London boards in Bayes; yes, I shall have no comparison against me. 'Egad, it's very hard that a gentleman, and an author can't come to teach them, but he must break his nose, and—and—all that—but—so the players are gone to dinner.'

Landlord: No such people frequent the Sun, I assure you.

Rover: 'Sun, moon, and stars!'—Now mind the eclipse, Mr Johnstone.

Landlord: I heard nothing of it, Sir.

Rover: 'There's the sun between the earth and moon—there's the moon between the earth and the sun, tol, lol, lol! dance the hay! Luna means to show her tail.'

    Enter **Waiter**.

Waiter: Two gentlemen in the parlour would speak with you, Sir.

Rover: 'I attend them, were they twenty times our mother.'

Landlord: Sir, you go in the stage; as we book the passengers, what name?

Rover: 'I am the bold Thunder.'

Landlord *(writing)*: Mr Thunder.

    Rover *exits. Enter* **John Dory**.

John: I want two places in the stage coach, because I and another gentleman are going a voyage.

Landlord: Just two vacant, what name?

John: Avast! I go aloft. But let's see who'll be my master's mess mates in the cabin: *(reads)* 'Captain Muccolah, Counsellor Fazacherly, Miss Gosling, Mr Thunder. What's this? Speak man! Is there one of that name going?

Landlord: Booked him this minute.

John: If our voyage should be at an end before we begin it?—if this Mr Thunder should be my master's son!—what rate is this vessel?

Landlord: Rate!—

John: What sort of a gentleman is he?

Landlord: Oh! a rum sort of a gentleman; I suspect he's one of the players.

John: True; Sam said it was some players' people coaxed him away from Portsmouth school. It must be the 'squire—show me where is he moored, my old purser.

    Exit, singing, and **Landlord** *following.*

SCENE THREE

A room in the Inn.
Lamp *and* **Trap** *(discovered drinking).*

Trap: This same Farmer Gammon seems a surly spark.

Lamp: No matter. His barn will hold a good thirty pounds and if I can but engage this young fellow, this Rover, he'll cram it every night he plays. He's certainly a very good actor. Now, Trap, you must inquire out a carpenter, and be brisk about the building. I think we shall have smart business, as we stand so well for pretty women too. Oh, here is Mr Rover!

Trap: Snap him at any terms.

Enter **Rover.**

Rover: Gentlemen, your most obedient—The waiter told me—

Lamp: Sir, to our better acquaintance. *(Fills)*

Rover: I don't recollect having the honour of knowing you.

Lamp: Mr Rover, though I am a stranger to you, your merit is none to me.

Rover: Sir! *(bows)*

Lamp: My name is Lamp; I am manager of the company of comedians that's come down here, and Mr Trap is my treasurer; engages performers, sticks bills, finds properties, keeps box-book, prompts plays and takes the towns.

Trap *(apart to* **Rover***):* The most reputable company, and charming money getting circuit.

Rover: I havn't a doubt, Sir.

Lamp: Only suffer me to put up your name to play with us six nights, and twelve guineas are yours.

Rover: Sir, I thank you, and must confess your offer is liberal;

but my friends have flattered me into a sort of opinion that encourages me to take a touch at the capital.

Lamp: Ah, my dear Mr Rover, a London Theatre is dangerous ground.

Rover: Why, I may fail, and gods may groan and ladies drawl, 'La, what an awkward creature!' But should I top my part, then shall gods applaud, and ladies sigh 'the charming fellow!' and managers take me by the hand, and treasurers smile upon me as they count the shining guineas!

Lamp: But, suppose—

Rover: Ah, suppose the contrary; I have a certain friend here, in my coat pocket. *(Puts his hand in his pocket) (aside)* Eh! where is—oh, the devil! I gave it to discharge my kind host—going for London, and not master of five shillings! 'Sir, to return to the twenty pounds.'

Lamp: Twenty pounds! Well, let it be so.

Rover: I engage with you; call a rehearsal, when and where you please, I'll attend.

Lamp: I'll step for the cast-book, and you shall choose your characters.

Trap: And, Sir, I'll write out the play-bills directly.

> *Exeunt* **Lamp** *and* **Trap**.

Rover: Since I must remain here some time, and I've not the most distant hope of ever speaking to this goddess again; I wish I had inquired her name, that I might know how to keep out of her way.

> *Enter* **John Dory** *and* **Landlord**.

Landlord: There's the gentleman.

John: Very well. *(Exit* **Landlord***)* What cheer, ho! master squire?

Rover: What cheer! my hearty!

John: The very face of his father! And ain't you asham'd of yourself?

Rover: Why, yes, I am sometimes.

John: Do you know, if I had you at the gangway, I'd give you a neater dozen than ever you got from your schoolmaster's cat-a-nine tails?

Rover: You wouldn't sure?

John: I would sure.

Rover: Indeed?—Pleasant enough! Who is this genius?

John: I've despatched a shallop to tell Lady Amaranth you're here.

Rover: You haven't?

John: I have.

Rover: Now, who the devil's Lady Amaranth.

John: I expect her chariot every moment, and when it comes, you'll get into it, and I'll get into it, and I'll set you down genteelly at her house; then I'll have obeyed my orders, and I hope your father will be satisfied.

Rover: My father! who's he, pray?

John: Pshaw! leave off your fun, and prepare to ask his pardon.

Rover: Ha, ha, ha! Why, my worthy friend, you are totally wrong in this affair. Upon my word I'm not the person you take me for. *(Going)*

John: You don't go, tho' they've got your name down in the stage coach book, Mr Thunder.

Rover: Mr Thunder! Stage coach book! *(Pauses)* Ha, ha, ha! This must be some curious blunder.

John: Oh! my lad, your father, Sir George, will change your note.

Rover: He must give me one first. Sir George! then my father is a knight it seems; ha, ha, ha! very good faith! 'pon my honour, I am not the gentleman that you think me.

John: I ought not to think you any gentleman for giving your honour in a falsehood. Oh! them play actors you went amongst have quite spoiled you. I wish only one of 'em would come in my way. I'd teach 'em to bring a gentleman's son tramboozing about the country.

Enter **Stage Coachman.**

Coach: Any passengers here for the balloon coach?

Rover: I was going; 'but by the care of standers by, prevented was.'

John: Ay; that was my care—I don't sail either, so you may weigh anchor without us.

Exit **Coachman.**

Enter **Waiter.**

Waiter: Her ladyship's chariot's at the door, and I fancy it's you, Sir, the coachman wants. *(Exit* **Waiter.***)*

John: Yes, it's me. I attend your honour.

Rover: Then you insist on it that I am—

John: I insist on nothing, only you shall come.

Rover: Indeed! Shall! 'Hear you this tritons of the minows? Mark you his absolute Shall?' Shall is a word, that does not sound over agreeable to my ears.

John: Does a pretty girl sound well to your ear?

Rover: 'More music in the clink of her horse's hoofs than twenty hautboys.' Why, is this Lady Thing-o-me, pretty?

John: Beautiful as a mermaid, and stately as a ship under sail.

Rover: A beautiful woman!—'Oh, such a sight! talk of a coronation.'

John: Coronation! zounds! what are you thinking of?

Rover: 'I was thinking of a side-saddle.'

John: Side-saddle! why, we go in the coach.

Rover *(aside)*: I've a mind to humour the frolic—Well, well, I'll see your mermaid. But then on the instant of my appearance the mistake must be discovered. Hearky, is this father of mine you talk of at this lady's?

John: No. Your father's in chase of the deserters. *(aside)* I find he's afraid to face the old one, so, if I tell him he won't go with me. No, no, we shan't see him in a hurry.

Rover: Then I'll venture. Has the lady ever seen me?

John: Pshaw! none of your jokes, man; you know that her ladyship, no more than myself, has set eyes upon you since you was the bigness of a Rumbo Canakin.

Rover: The choice is made. I have my Ranger's dress, in my trunk, 'Cousin of Buckingham, thou sage, grave man!'

John: What?

Rover: 'Since you will buckle fortune on my back, to bear her burden, whether I will or no, I must have patience to endure the load? but if black scandal or foul faced'—

John: Black! my foul face was as fair as yours before I went to sea.

Rover: 'Your mere enforcement shall acquittance me.'

John: Man, don't stand preaching parson Palmer—come to the chariot.

Rover: Ay, to the chariot! 'Bear me, Bucephalus, among the billows,—hey! for the Tigris!'

Exeunt.

END OF THE SECOND ACT

ACT THREE

SCENE ONE

Lady Amaranth's house.
Enter **Lady Amaranth,** *and* **Ephraim Smooth.**

Lady Amaranth: Tho' thou hast settled that distressed
gentleman's debt, let his sister come unto me, and remit a
quarter's rent unto all my tenants.

Ephraim: As thou biddest, I have discharged from the pound
the widow's cattle; but shall I let the lawsuit drop against the
farmer's son, who did shoot the pheasant?

Lady Amaranth: Yea; but instantly turn from my service the
gamekeeper's man that did kill the fawn, while it was eating
from his hand. We should hate guile, tho' we may love
venison.

Ephraim *(aside)*: I love a young doe. Since the death of friend
Dovehouse, who, tho' one of the faithful, was an active
magistrate, this part of the country is infested with covetous
men, called robbers, and I have in thy name said unto the
people, whoever apprehendeth one of these, I will reward
him, yea with thirty pieces of gold. *(A loud knocking
without)* That beating of one brass against another at thy
door, proclaimeth the approach of vanity whose pride of
heart swelleth at an empty sound. *(Exit)*

Lady Amaranth: But my heart is possessed with the idea of that
wandering youth, whose benevolence induced him to part
with (perhaps) his all, to free the unhappy debtor. His person
is amiable, his address (according to worldly modes) formed
to please, to delight. But he's poor: is that a crime? Perhaps
meanly born; but one good act is an illustrious pedigree. I

feel I love him, and in that word are contained birth, fame, and riches.

Enter Jane.

Jane: Madam, my lady, an't please you.—

Lady Amaranth: Didst thou find the young man, that I may return him the money he paid for my tenant?

Jane: I found him ma'am, and—I found him, and he talk'd of—what he said.

Lady Amaranth: What did he say?

Jane: He saw me, ma'am—and call'd me Blowsabella, and said he would—I'll be hang'd, ma'am, if he didn't say he would—Now, think of that—but if he hadn't gone to London in the stagecoach.

Lady Amaranth: Is he gone? *(with emotion)*

Enter John Dory.

John: Oh, my lady, mayhap John Dory is not the man to be sent after young gentlemen that scamper from school, and run about the country play acting! *(Calls off)* Pray walk upstairs, Master Thunder.

Lady Amaranth: Hast thou brought my kinsman hither?

John: Well, I hav'n't then.

Jane: If you hav'n't, why do you make such a talk about it?

John: Don't give me your palaver.—Will you only walk up, if you please, Master Harry?

Jane: Will you walk up if you please, Master Harry?

Lady Amaranth *(aside)*: Friendship requireth, yet I am not disposed to commune with company.

Jane: Oh, bless me, ma'am! If it isn't—

Enter Rover, *dressed.*

Rover: 'Tis I, Hamlet the Dane!'—'Thus far, into the bowels of the land, have we march'd on.'—'John, that bloody and devouring boar!'

John: He called me bull in the coach.

Jane: I don't know what brought such a bull into the coach!

Rover: This the Lady Amaranth! By heavens, the very angel quaker!

Lady Amaranth *(turns)*: The dear, generous youth, my cousin Harry!

John: There he's for you, my lady, and make the most of him.

Jane: Oh, how happy my lady is! he looks so charming now he's fine.

John *(apart to* **Rover***)*: Harky! she's as rich as a Spanish India-man, and I tell you, your father wishes you'd grapple her by the heart—court her, you mad devil. *(to* **Jane***)* There's an engagement to be between these two vessels; but little cupid's the only man that's to take minutes, so come.

Jane: Ma'am, an't I to wait on you?

John: No, my lass, you're to wait on me.

Jane: Wait on this great sea-bull! am I—ma'am?

John *(aside)*: By this, Sir George is come to the inn,—without letting the younker know I'll go and bring him here, and smuggle both father and son into a joyful meeting. *(to* **Jane***)* Come now, usher me down like a lady.

Jane: This way, Mr Sailor Gentleman.

    Exeunt, **John** *and* **Jane.**

Rover *(aside)*: By heavens, a most delectable woman!

Lady Amaranth: Cousin, when I saw thee in the village free the sheep from the wolf, why didst not tell me then thou wert son to my uncle, Sir George?

Rover: Because, my lady, then I—*(aside)* didn't know it myself.

Lady Amaranth: Why would'st thou vex thy father, and quit thy school.

Rover: 'A truant disposition, good, my lady, brought me from Wirtemburg.'

Lady Amaranth: Thy father designs thee for his dangerous profession; but is thy inclination turned to the voice of trumpets, and smites of mighty slaughter?

Rover: 'Why, ma'am, as for old Boreas, my dad, when the blast of war blows in his ears, he's a tiger in his fierce resentment.'—But for me, 'I think it a pity, and so it is, that villainous saltpetre should be digg'd out of the bowels of the harmless earth, which many a good tall fellow has destroyed, with wounds and guns, and drums, heav'n save the mark!'

Lady Amaranth: Indeed thou art tall, my cousin, and grown of comely stature. Our families have long been separated.

Rover: They have.—*(aside)* Since Adam, I believe—'Then, lady, let that sweet bud of love now ripen to a beauteous flower!'

Lady Amaranth: Love!

Rover: 'Excellent lady! perdition catch my soul, but I do love thee, and when I love thee not, Chaos is come again.'

Lady Amaranth: Thou art of an happy disposition.

Rover: 'If I were now to die, 'twere now to be most happy. Let our senses dance in concert to the joyful minutes, and this and this the only discord make.' *(kisses her hand)*

Enter **Jane**, *with cake and wine.*

Jane: Ma'am, an't please you, Mr Zachariah bid me—

Rover: 'Why, you fancy yourself Cardinal Wolsey in this family.'

Jane: No, sir, I'm not a Cardinal, I'm only my lady's maid here—Jenny Gammon, at your service.

Rover: 'A bowl of cream for your Catholic Majesty.'

Jane: Cream! La, Sir, it's wine and water.

Rover: 'You get no water, take the wine, great Potentate.' *(Presents a glass to* **Lady Amaranth***)*

Jane: Madam, my father begs leave—

Rover: 'Go, go, thou shallow Pomona.' *(Puts her out)* Eh, s'death! my manager!

Enter **Farmer Gammon**, *and* **Lamp**.

F. Gammon *(aside)*: I hope her ladyship hasn't found out 'twas I had Banks arrested.—Would your ladyship give leave for this here honest man and his comrade to act a few plays in the town, 'cause I've let'n my barn. 'Twill be some little help to me my lady.

Rover: I understand more of these affairs than ladies do. Leave me to settle 'em, madam.

Lady Amaranth: True; these are delusions, as a woman, I understand not. But by my cousin's advice I will abide; ask his permission.

Gammon *(aside)*: So; I must pay my respects to the young Squire. An't please your honour, if a poor man like me *(bows)* durst offer my humble duty—

Rover: 'Canst thou bow to a Vagrant.' Eh, Little Hospitality?

Farmer Gammon *looks at him and sneaks off.*

Lamp: Please your honour, if I may presume to hope you'll be graciously pleased to take our little squad under your honour's protection.

Rover: Ha!

Lady Amaranth: What say'st thou, Henry?

Rover: Ay, where's Henry? *(aside)* True, that's me. Strange I should already forget my name, and not half an hour since I was christened! Hark! do you play yourself? Eh! Ha! Hem! fellow?

Lamp: Yes, Sir; and Sir, I have just now engaged a new actor, one Mr Rover. Such an actor! but I dare say, Sir, you've heard of Mr Rover.

Rover: Eh! What! you've engaged that—what's his name, Rover? If such is your best actor, you shan't have my permission. My dear madam, the worst fellow in the world. Get along out of the town, or I'll have all of you, man, woman, child, stick, rag, and fiddlestick, clapt into the whirligig.

Lady Amaranth: Good man, abide not here.

Rover: Eh! What my friend? Now, indeed, if this new actor you brag of, this crack of your company, was anything like a gentleman.

Lamp *(surprised)*: It isn't!

Rover: It is. My good friend, if I was really the unfortunate poor strolling dog you thought me, I should tread your four boards, and crow the cock of your barndoor fowl; but as fate has ordained that I'm a gentleman, and son to Sir,—Sir, *(aside)* what the devil's my father's name? you must be content to murder Shakespeare without making me an accomplice.

Lamp: But, my most gentle Sir, I, and my treasurer, Tråp, have trumpeted your fame ten miles round the country:—the bills are posted, the stage built, the candles book'd, fiddles engaged; all on the tip-top of expectation. We should have tomorrow night an overflow, ay, thirty pounds. Dear, worthy Sir, you wouldn't go to ruin a whole community and their families, that now depend only on the exertion of your brilliant talents.

Rover: Eh! I never was uniform but in one maxim, that is, tho' I do little good, to hurt nobody but myself.

Lady Amaranth: Since thou hast promised, much as I prize my adherance to those customs in which I was brought up, thou shalt not sully thy honour by a breach of thy word; for truth is more shining than beaten gold. Play, if it can bring good to these people.

Rover: Shall I?

Lady Amaranth: This falleth out well; for I have bidden all the wealthy people round unto my house-warming, and these pleasantries may afford them a cheerful and innocent entertainment.

Rover: True, my lady; your guests an't quakers tho' you are; and when we ask people to our house, we study to please them, not ourselves. But if we do furnish up a play or two, the muses shan't honour that churlish fellow's barn. The God that illumines the soul of genius should never visit the iron door of inhumanity. No Gammon's barn for me!—

Lady Amaranth: Barn! that gallery shall be thy theatre; and, in spite of the grave doctrines of Ephraim Smooth, my friends and I will behold and rejoice in thy pranks, my pleasant cousin.

Rover: My kind, my charming lady! Hey, brighten up, bully Lamp, carpenters, tailor, manager, distribute your box tickets for my lady's gallery.—'Come, gentle coz,'

'The actors are at hand and by their show
You shall know all
That you are like to know.'

Exeunt.

SCENE TWO

The Inn.
Enter **Harry**, *in a riding dress, and* **Muz** *in a Livery.*

Harry: Tho' I went back to Portsmouth academy with a contrite heart to continue my studies; yet, from my father's angry letter, I dread a woeful storm at our first meeting. I fancy the people at this inn don't recollect me; it reminds me of my pleasant friend, poor Jack Rover; I wonder where he is now.

Muz: And it brings to my memory a certain stray-vaguing acquaintance of mine, poor Dick Buskin.

Harry: Ha, ha, ha! Then I desire, Sir, you'll turn Dick Buskin again out of your memory.

Muz: Can't sir. The dear, good natur'd, wicked—beg your honour's pordon.

Harry: Oh, but Muz, you must, as soon as I'm dress'd, step out and inquire whose house is this my father's at; I did not think he had any acquaintance in this part of the country. Sound what humour he's in, and how the land lies before I venture in his presence.

Enter **Waiter.**

Waiter: Sir, the room is ready for you to dress. *(Exit)*

Harry: I shall only throw off my boots, and you'll shake a little powder in my hair.

Muz: Then, hey, puff, I shoulder my curling irons.

Exeunt.

Enter **Sir George Thunder** *and* **Landlord.**

Sir George: I can hear nothing of these deserters; yet, by my first intelligence, they'll not venture up to London. They must

35

still be lurking about the country. Landlord, have any suspicious persons put in at your house?

Landlord: Yes, sir; now and then.

Sir George: What do you do with them?

Landlord: Why, Sir, when a man calls for liquor, that I think has no money, I make him pay before hand.

Sir George: Damn your liquor, you self-interested porpoise! Chatter your own private concerns, when the public good, or fear of general calamity should be the only compass. These fellows that I'm in pursuit of, have run from their ships; if our navy's unmann'd, what becomes of you and your house, you cormorant?

Landlord *(aside)*: This is a very abusive sort of gentleman; but he has a full pocket, or he wouldn't be so saucy. *(Exit)*

Sir George: This rascal, I believe, doesn't know I'm Sir George Thunder. Winds still variable, blow my affairs right athwart each other.—To know what's become of my runagate son Harry, and there my rich lady niece, pressing and squeezing up the noble plumage of our illustrious family in her little mean quaker bonnet; but I must up to town after—S'blood, when I catch my son Harry!—Oh, here's John Dory.

Enter **John Dory.**

Have you taken the places in the London coach for me?

John: Hahoy! your honour, is that yourself?

Sir George: No, I'm beside myself—heard anything of my son?—

John: What's o'clock?

Sir George: What do you talk of clocks or timepieces—All glasses reck'ning, and log-line are run wild with me.

John: If it's two, your son is at this moment walking with Lady Amaranth in her garden.

Sir George: With Lady Amaranth!

John: If half after, they're cast anchor to rest themselves amongst the posies; if three, they're got up again; if four, they're picking a bit of cramm'd fowl; and, if half after, they're cracking walnuts over a bottle of Calcavella.

Sir George: My son! my dear friend, where did you find him?

John: Why, I found him where he was, and I left him where he is.

Sir George: What, and he came to Lady Amaranth's?

John: No; but I brought him there from this house in her ladyship's chariot. *(aside)* I won't tell him master Harry went amongst the players, or he'd never forgive him . . . Oh! such a merry, civil, crazy, crackbrain! the very picture of your honour.

Sir George: Ha, ha, ha! What, he's in high spirits? ha, ha, ha! the dog! *(joyfully)*. But I hope he had discretion enough to throw a little gravity over his mad humour, before his prudent cousin.

John: He threw himself on his knees before her, and that did quite as well.

Sir George: Ha, ha, ha! made love to her already! Oh, the impudent, the cunning villain! What, and may be he—

John: Indeed he did give her a smack.

Sir George: Me; ha, ha ha!

John: Oh, he's your's! a chip of the old block.

Sir George: He is! he is! ha, ha, ha!

John: Oh, he threw his arms around her, as eager as I would to catch a falling decanter of Madeira.

Sir George: Huzza! Victoria! Here will be a junction of two bouncing estates! but, confound the money. John you shall have a bowl for a jolly boat to swim in; roll in here a puncheon of rum, a hogshead of sugar, shake an orchard of oranges, and let the landlord drain his fishpond yonder. *(Sings)* 'A bumper! a bumper of good liquor.'

John: Then my good master, Sir George, I'll order a bowl in, since you are in the humour for it—'We'll dance a little, and sing a little.' *(Exit singing)*

Sir George: And so the wild rogue is this instant rattling up her prim ladyship. Eh, isn't this he? Left her already!

    Enter **Harry** *dressed.*

Harry: I must have forgot my cane in this room—My father!

Sir George *(looks at his watch)*: Just half after four! Why, Harry, you've made great haste in cracking your walnuts.

Harry: Yes; *(aside)* he's heard of my frolics with the players. Dear father, if you'll but forgive—

Sir George: Why indeed, Harry, your running away was not well—I've heard all, you've acted very bad.

Harry: Sir, it should be considered I was but a novice.

Sir George: However, I shall think of nothing now but your benefit.

Harry *(aside)*: Very odd his approving of—I suppose he means to let me have my frolic out. I thank you, Sir, but, if agreeable to you, I've done with benefits.

Sir George: If I wasn't the best of fathers, you might indeed hope for none; but no matter, if you can get but the Fair Quaker.

Harry: Or, The Humours of the Navy, Sir?

Sir George: What! how dare you reflect on the humours of the navy? The navy has very good humours, or I'd never see your dog's face again, you villain! But I'm cool,—Eh, boy, a snug easy chariot?

Harry: I'll order it. *(Calls off)* Waiter, desire my father's carriage to draw up.

Sir George: Mine, you rogue! I've none here. I mean Lady Amaranth's.

Harry: Yes Sir, *(calling off)* Lady Amaranth's chariot!

Sir George: What are you at? I mean that which you left this house in.

Harry: Chariot! Sir, I left this house on foot.

Sir George: What, with John Dory?

Harry: No, Sir, with Jack Rover.

Sir George: Why, John has been a rover to be sure; but now he's settled since I've made him my valet de chambre.

Harry: Make him your valet! Why, Sir, where did you meet him?

Sir George: I met him on board, and I met him on shore, the cabin, steerage, galley, and forecastle. He sailed round the world with me.

Harry: Strange this Sir! Certainly I understood he had been in the East Indies; but he never told me he even knew you; but, indeed, he knew me only by the name of Dick Buskin.

Sir George: Then how came he to bring you to Lady Amaranth's?

Harry: Bring me where, Sir?

Sir George: Answer me, are not you now come from her Ladyship's?

Harry: Me? Not I.

Sir George: Ha! this is a lie of John's to enhance his own services. Then, you have not been there?

Harry: There! I don't know where you mean, Sir.

Sir George: Yes; 'tis all a brag of John's, but I'll—

    Enter **John Dory.**

John: The rum and sugar is ready; but as for the fishpond—

Sir George: I'll kick you into it, you thirsty old grampus.

John: Will you? Then I'll make a comical roasted orange.

Sir George: How dare you say you brought my son to Lady Amaranth's.

John: And who says I did not?

Sir George (*ironically*): He that best should know; only Dick Buskin here.

John: Then, Dick Buskin might find some other amusement than shooting off his guns here.

Sir George: Did you bring my son to Lady Amaranth's in her chariot?

John: And to be sure I did.

Sir George: There, what do you say to that?

Harry: I say it's false.

John: False! Shiver my hulk, Mr Buckskin, if you wore a lion's skin, I'd curry you for this. *(Exit in a rage)*

Sir George: No, no, John's honest, I see thro' it now. The puppy has seen her, perhaps he has the impudence not to like her, and so blows up this confusion and perplexity only to break off a marriage that I've set my heart on.

Harry (*aside*): What does he mean? Sir, I'll assure you—

Sir George: Damn your assurance, you disobedient, ungrateful—I'll not part with you 'till I confront you with Lady Amaranth herself face to face, and if I prove you've been deceiving me, I'll launch you into the wide ocean of life without rudder, compass, grog, or tobacco.

    Exeunt.

END OF THE THIRD ACT

ACT FOUR

SCENE ONE

Lady Amaranth's *House.*
Enter **Lady Amaranth,** *reading.*

Lady Amaranth: The fanciful flights of my pleasant cousin enchant my senses. This book he gave me to read containeth good moral. The man Shakespeare, that did write it, they call immortal; he must indeed have been filled with a divine spirit. I understand, from my cousin, the origin of plays were religious mysteries; that, freed from the superstition of early, and the grossness of latter ages, the stage is now the vehicle of delight and morality. If so, to hear a good play, is taking the wholesome draught of precept from a golden cup, emboss'd with gems; yet, my giving countenance to have one in my house, and even to act in it myself prove the ascendancy that my dear Harry hath over my heart—Ephraim Smooth is much scandalized at these doings.

    Enter **Ephraim Smooth.**

Ephraim: This mansion is now the tabernacle of Baal.

Lady Amaranth: Then abide not in it.

Ephraim: 'Tis full of the wicked ones.

Lady Amaranth: Stay not amongst the wicked ones.

    Loud laughing without.

Ephraim: I must shut mine ears.

Lady Amaranth: And thy mouth also, good Ephraim. I have bidden my cousin Henry to my house, and I will not set bounds to his mirth to gratify thy spleen, and show mine own inhospitality.

Ephraim: Why dost thou suffer him to put into the hands of thy

40

servants books of tragedies, and books of comedies, prelude, interlude, yea, all lewd. My spirit doth wax wrath. I say unto thee, a play house is the school for the old dragon, and a play book, the primer of Belzebub.

Lady Amaranth: This is one; mark! *(Reads)* 'Not the King's crown, nor the deputed sword, the marshal's truncheon, nor the judge's robe, become them with one half so good a grace as mercy doth. Oh, think on that, and mercy then will breathe within your lips like man new made!' Doth Beelzebub speak such words?

Ephraim: Thy kinsman hath made all thy servants actors.

Lady Amaranth: To act well is good service.

Ephraim *(aside)*: Here cometh the damsel for whom my heart yearneth.

    Enter **Jane,** *reading.*

Jane: Oh, Ma'am, his honour the squire, says the play's to be 'As You Like It.'

Ephraim: I like it not.

Jane: He's given me my character. I'm to be Miss Audrey, and brother Sim's to be William of the forest as it were. But how am I to get my part by heart?

Lady Amaranth: By often reading it.

Jane: Well, I don't know but that's as good a way as any. But I must study it. 'The gods give us joy.' *(Exit)*

Ephraim: Thy maidens skip like young kids.

Lady Amaranth: Then do thou go skip with them.

Ephraim: Mary, thou shou'd'st be obeyed in thine own house, and I will do thy bidding.

Lady Amaranth: Ah, thou hypocrite! To obey is easy when the heart commands.

    Enter **Rover.**

Rover: Oh, my charming cousin, how agree you and Rosalind? Are you almost perfect? 'Eh, what, all a-mort, old Clytus?' 'Why, you're like an angry fiend broke in among the laughing gods.'—Come, come, I'll have nothing here, but, 'quips and cranks and wreathed smiles, such as dwell on Hebe's cheek.' *(Looking at* **Lady Amaranth***)*

Lady Amaranth: He says we mustn't have this amusement.

Rover: 'But I'm a voice potential, double as the Duke's, and I say we must.'

Ephraim: Nay.

Rover: Yea: 'By Jupiter, I swear, aye.'

Music without.

Ephraim: I must shut my ears. The man of sin rubbeth the hair of the horse to the bowels of the cat.

Enter **Lamp,** *with a violin.*

Lamp: Now, if agreeable to your Ladyship, we'll go over your song.

Ephraim: I will go over it. *(Snatches the book from* **Lady Amaranth,** *throws it on the ground, and steps on it)*

Rover: Trample on Shakespeare! 'A sacrilegious thief, that, from a shelf the precious diadem stole, and put it in his pocket!' *(Takes up the book and presents it to* **Lady Amaranth)** Silence, 'thou owl of Crete,' and hear the 'Cuckoo's song'.

Lady Amaranth: To practice it I'm content.

Lamp begins to play. **Ephraim** *jostles him, and puts him out of tune.*

Lamp: Why, what's that for, my dear sir?

Ephraim: Friend, this a land of freedom, and I've as much right to move my elbow, as thou hast to move thine.

Rover *pushes him.*

Why dost thou so friend?

Rover: 'Friend, this is a land of freedom, and I have as much right to move my elbow, as thou hast to move thine. *(shoves* **Ephraim** *out)* 'Verily, I could smite that Amalekite 'till the going down of the sun.'

Lady Amaranth: But, Harry, do your people of fashion act these follies themselves.

Rover: Ay, and scramble for the top parts as eager as for star, ribband, place or pension; and no wonder, for a good part in a play is the first good character some of them ever had. Lamp, decorate the seats out smart and theatrical, and drill the servants that I've given the small parts to—

Exit **Lamp.**

Lady Amaranth: I wished for some entertainment, (in which gay people now take delight) to please those I have invited; but we'll convert these follies into a charitable purpose. Tickets for this day shall be delivered unto my friends gratis; but money to their amount, I will, (after rewarding our assistants) distribute amongst the indigent of the village. Thus, whilst we please ourselves, and perhaps amuse our friends, we shall make the poor happy. *(Exit)*.

Rover: An angel! If Sir George doesn't soon arrive to blow me, I may, I think, marry her angelic ladyship; but will that be honest; she's nobly born, though I suspect I had ancestors too if I knew who they were. I certainly entered this house the poorest wight in England, and what must she imagine when I am discovered? That I am a scoundrel; and, consequently, tho' I should possess her hand and fortune, instead of loving, she'll despise me—*(sits)* I want a friend now, to consult—deceive her I will not. Poor Dick Buskin wants money more than myself, yet this is a measure I'm sure he'd scorn. No, no, I must not.

    Enter **Harry**.

Harry: Now I hope my passionate father will be convinced this is the first time I was ever under this roof. Eh, what beau is here? Astonishing! My old strolling friend! *(Unperceived, sits by* **Rover***)*

Rover: Heigho! I don't know what to do.

Harry *(in the same tone)*: 'Nor what to say.'

Rover *(turns)*: Dick Buskin! My dear fellow! Ha, ha, ha! Talk of the devil, and—I was just thinking of you—'pon my soul, Dick, I'm so happy to see you.

    Shakes hands cordially.

Harry: But, Jack, eh, perhaps you found me out.

Rover: Found you! I'm sure I wonder how the deuce you found me out. Ah, the news of my intended play has brought you.

Harry *(aside)*: He doesn't know as yet who I am, so I'll carry it on. Then you too have broke your engagement with Truncheon at Winchester; figuring it away in your stage clothes too. Really tell us what you are at here, Jack.

Rover: Will you be quiet with your Jacking? I'm now Squire Harry.

Harry: What?

Rover: I've been pressed into this service by an old man of war, who found me at the inn, and, insisting I'm son to a Sir George Thunder, here, in that character, I flatter myself I have won the heart of the charming lady of this house.

Harry: Now the mystery's out. *(aside)* Then it's my friend Jack has been brought here for me. Do you know the young gentleman they take you for?

Rover: No; but I'm proud to say he is honoured in his representative.

Harry: Upon my soul, Jack, you're a very high fellow. Ha, ha, ha!

Rover: I am, now I can put some pounds in your pocket; you shall be employed—we're getting up 'As You Like It'. Let's see, in the cast, have I a part for you—I'll take Touchstone from Lamp, you shall have it, my boy; I'd resign Orlando to you with any other Rosalind: but the lady of the mansion plays it herself.

Harry *(aside)*: The very lady my father intended for me. Do you love her, Jack?

Rover: To distraction; but I'll not have her.

Harry: No! Why?

Rover: She thinks me a gentleman, and I'll not convince her I'm a rascal. I'll go on with our play, as the produce is appropriate to a good purpose, and then lay down my squireship, bid adieu to my heavenly Rosalind, and exit for ever from her house, poor Jack Rover.

Harry *(aside)*: The generous fellow I ever thought him and he sha'nt lose by it. If I could make him believe—*(pauses)* Ha, ha, ha! Well, this is the most whimsical affair! You've anticipated, superseded me, ha, ha, ha! You'll scarce believe that I'm come here too (purposely though) to pass myself for this young Harry.

Rover: No!

Harry: I am.

Sir George *(without)*: Harry, where are you?

Rover: Eh! Who's that?

Harry: Ha, ha, ha! *(aside)* I'll try it, my father will be cursedly vexed; but no other way.

Rover: Somebody called Harry—'if the real Simon Pure' should be arrived, I'm in a fine way.

Harry: Be quiet—that's my confederate.

Rover: Eh!

Harry: He's to personate the father, Sir George Thunder. He started the scheme having heard that a union was intended, and Sir George not immediately expected—our plan is, if I can, before his arrival, flourish myself into the lady's good graces, and whip her up, as she's an heiress.

Rover: But who is this comrade?

Harry: One of my former company, a devilish good actor in the old men.

Rover: So, you're turned fortune hunter! Oh ho! then twas on this plan that you parted with me on the road, standing like a finger post, 'you walk up that way, and I walk down this'. Why Dick, I didn't know you were half so capital a rogue.

Harry: I didn't know my forte lay that way, 'till persuaded by this experienced stager.

Rover: He must be an impudent old scoundrel; who is he? Do I know him?

Harry *(aside)*: Why, no—I hope not.

Rover: I'll step down-stairs, and have the honour of—I'll kick him.

Harry: No, I wouldn't have him hurt either.

Rover: What's his name?

Harry: His name is—is—Abrawang.

Rover: Abrawang! I never heard of him, but, Dick, why would you let him persuade you to such a scandalous affair?

Harry: Why faith, I would have been off it; but when once he takes a project into his head, the devil himself can't drive him out of it.

Rover: Yes; but the constable may drive him into Winchester gaol.

Harry: Eh! Your opinion of our intended exploit has made me ashamed of myself—ha, ha, ha! Harkey, Jack, to frighten and punish my adviser, do you still keep your character of young squire Thunder—you can easily do that, as he, no more than myself, has ever seen the young gentleman.

Rover: But by Heavens I'll—'Quoit him down, Bardolph'.

Harry: Yes, but, Jack, if you can marry her, her fortune is a snug thing; besides if you love each other,—I tell you—

Rover: Hang her fortune! 'My love more noble than the world, prizes not quantity of dirty lands.' Oh, Dick, she is the most lovely—but you shall see her, she is female beauty in its genuine decoration. *(Exit)*

Harry: Ha, ha, ha! this is the drollest—Rover little suspects that I am the identical Squire Thunder that he personates.—I'll lend him my character a little longer.—Yes, this offers a most excellent opportunity of making my poor friend's fortune, without injuring anybody; if possible he shall have her. I can't regret the loss of charms I never knew, and, as for an estate, my father's is competent to all my wishes. Lady Amaranth, by marrying Jack Rover, will gain a man of honour, which she might miss in an earl—it may tease my father a little at first, but he's a good old fellow in the main, and, I think, when he comes to know my motive—Eh! this must be she—an elegant woman faith! Now for a little finesse, to continue her in the belief that Jack is the man she thinks him. Madam, a word if you please. *(bowing)*

Enter **Lady Amaranth**.

Lady Amaranth: Who art thou, friend?

Harry: I've scarce time to warn you against the danger you are in of being imposed upon by your Uncle, Sir George.

Lady Amaranth: How?

Harry: He has heard of your ladyship's partiality for his son; but is so incensed at the irregularity of his conduct, that he intends, if possible, to disinherit him; and to prevent your honouring him with your hand, has engaged me, and brought me hither, to pass me on you for him, designing to treat the poor young gentleman himself as an imposter, in hopes you'll banish him your heart and house.

Lady Amaranth: Is Sir George such a parent? I thank thee for thy caution.—What is thy name!

Harry: Richard Buskin, ma'am; the stage is my profession. In the young squire's late excursion, we contracted an intimacy, and I saw so many good qualities in him, that I could not think of being the instrument of his ruin, nor deprive your ladyship of so good a husband, as I'm certain he'll make you.

Lady Amaranth: Then Sir George intends to disown him?

Harry: Yes, ma'am; I've this moment told the young gentleman of it; and he's determined, for a jest, to return the compliment, by seeming to treat Sir George himself as an imposter.

Lady Amaranth: 'Twill be a just retaliation, and, indeed, what my uncle deserveth for his cruel intentions both to his son and me.

Sir George *(without)*: What, has he run away again?

Lady Amaranth: That's mine uncle.

Harry *(aside):* Yes, here is my father; and my standing out that I am not his son, will rouse him into the heat of battle, ha, ha, ha! Here he is, madam, now mind how he will dub me 'squire.

Lady Amaranth: It's well I'm prepared, or I might have believed him.

   Enter **Sir George**.

Sir George: Well, my lady, wasn't it my wild rogue set you to all the Calcavella capers you've been cutting in the garden? You see here I have brought him into the line of battle again—you villain, why do you drop astern there? Throw a salute-shot, buss her bob-stays, bring to, and come down straight as a mast, you dog.

Lady Amaranth: Uncle, who is this?

Sir George: Who is he—Ha, ha, ha! That's an odd question to the fellow that has been three hours with you cracking walnuts.

Lady Amaranth: He is bad at his lesson.

Sir George: Certainly, when he ran away from school—why don't you speak, you lubber? you're curst modest now, but before I came, 'twas all down amongst the posies—Here, my lady, take from a father's hand, Harry Thunder.

Lady Amaranth: That is what I may not.

Sir George: There, I thought you'd disgust her, you flat fish!
   Enter **Rover**.

Lady Amaranth *(taking* **Rover**'s *hand)*: Here Uncle, take from my hand, Harry Thunder.

Sir George: Eh! *(Staring at* **Rover**)

Rover *(apart to* **Harry**): Oh! this is our sham Sir George?

Harry *(apart to* **Rover**): Yes; I've been telling the lady, and she'll seem to humour him.

Rover: I sha'nt though. How do you do, Abrawang?

Sir George: Abrawang!

Rover: You look like a good actor.—Ay, that's very well, indeed—never lose sight of your character—you know, Sir George Thunder is a noisy, turbulent, wicked old seaman.—Angry! bravo!—pout your underlip, purse your brows—very well! But, dem it, Abrawang, you should have put a little red upon your nose—mind a rule, ever play an angry old man, with a red nose. That's right! Strut about on your little pegs.

Sir George: I'm in such a fury!

Rover: We know that. Your figure is the most happy comedy squab I ever saw, why only show yourself, and you set the audience in a roar.

Sir George: S'blood and fire!

Rover: 'Keep it up, I like fun.'

Lady Amaranth: Who is this!
    To **Sir George**, *pointing to* **Rover**.

Sir George: Some puppy unknown.

Lady Amaranth: And you don't know this gentleman?
    To **Rover**, *pointing to* **Sir George**.

Rover: Excellently well. 'He's a fishmonger.'

Sir George: A what?

Lady Amaranth: Yes, father and son are determined not to know each other.

Rover: Come Dick, give the lady a specimen of your talents, 'Motley's your only wear, ha, ha, ha! I met a fool in the forest'.

Harry: Here comes Audrey, 'Salutation and greeting to you all, Trip, trip, apace, good Audrey.'
    Enter **Jane**, **Harry** *takes her arm under his, they trip round, then go up to* **Sir George**.

Jane *(to Sir George)*: 'La! warrants, what features!'

Sir George: S'blood, what's this?

Harry: 'A homely thing, Sir, but she's mine own.'

Sir George: Your's? Oh, you most audacious—what, this slut?

Jane: 'I thank the Gods for my sluttishness.'

Lady Amaranth *(to Rover, pointing at Harry)*: You know this youth?

Rover: 'My friend, Horatio'—'I wear him in my heart's core, yea, in my heart of hearts,' as I do thee. *(kisses her hand)*

Sir George: Such freedom with my niece before my face! Do you know that lady, do you know my son, Sir?

Rover: Be quiet. 'Jaffier has discover'd the plot, and you can't deceive the Senate.'

Harry: Yes, my conscience wouldn't let me carry it thro'.

Rover: 'Ay, his conscience hanging about the neck of his heart, says, good Launcelot, and good Gobbo, as aforesaid, good Launcelot Gobbo, take to thy heels and run.'

Sir George: Why, my Lady! explain, scoundrel, and puppy unknown.

Lady Amaranth: Uncle, I've heard thy father was kind to thee, return that kindness to thy child. If the lamb in wanton play doth fall among the waters, the shepherd taketh him out, instead of plunging him deeper till he dieth. Tho' thy hairs now be gray, I'm told they were once flaxen; in short, he is too old in folly, who cannot excuse it in youth. *(Exit)*

Sir George: I'm an old fool! Well, that's civil of you, Madam niece, and I'm a grey shepherd—with her visions and her vines, and her lambs in a ditch; but as for you, young Mr Goat, I'll butt you—

Rover: My dear, Abrawang, give up the game—her Ladyship, in seeming to take you for her uncle, has been only humming you! What the devil, don't you think the fine creature knows her own trueborn uncle?

Sir George: Certainly; to be sure she knows me.

Rover: Will you have done? Zounds, man, my honour'd father was here himself to-day—Her Ladyship knows his person.

Sir George: Your honoured father! And who's your honour'd self?

Rover: 'Now by my father's son, and that's myself, it shall be sun, moon, or a Cheshire cheese—before I budge—still crossed and crossed.'

Sir George: What do you bawl out to me of Cheshire cheeses, I say—

Rover: 'And I say, as the saying is'—your friend, Dick, has told me all; but to convince you of my forgiveness, in our play, as you're a rough and tough, I'll cast you Charles the Wrestler, I do Orlando; I'll trip up your heels before the whole court.

Sir George: Trip up my heels! Why, damme, I'll—And you, you undutiful chick of an old pelican—

Lifting up his cane to strike **Harry**. *Enter* **John** *who receives the blow.*

John: What are you at here? Cudgelling the people about? But Mr Buckskin, I've a word to say to you in private.

Sir George: Buckskin!

Enter **Lamp** *and* **Trap**, *and two* **female servants**.

Lamp: 'All the world's a stage, and all the men and women—'

Sir George: The men are rogues, and the women hussies—I'll make a clear stage.

Beats them off—and amongst the rest, strikes **Rover**.

Rover: 'A blow! Essex a blow'—An old rascally imposter stigmatize me with a blow—no, I must not put up with it.—Zounds! I shall be tweak'd by the nose all round the country—I'll follow him. 'Strike me! So may this arm dash him to the earth, like a dead dog despised—blindness and leprosy, lameness and lunacy, pride, shame, and the name of villain light on me if I don't'—bang—Mr Abrawang.

Exit.

SCENE TWO

Another Apartment.
Enter **Lady Amaranth** *and* **Banks**.

Banks: Madam, I could have paid the rent of my little cottage; but I daresay it was without your ladyship's knowledge that your steward has turn'd me out, and put my neighbour in possession.

Lady Amaranth: My steward oppress the poor! I did not know it indeed friend.

Banks: The pangs of adversity I could bear; but the innocent partner of my misfortunes, my unhappy sister—

Lady Amaranth: I did desire Ephraim to send for thy sister.—Did she dwell with thee, and both now without a home? Let her come to mine.

Banks: The hand of misery has struck us beneath your notice!

Lady Amaranth: Thou dost mistake—To need my assistance is the highest claim to my attention; let me see her—
  Exit **Banks**.
I could chide myself that these pastimes have turned my eye from the house of woe. Ah! think, ye proud and happy affluent, how many in your dancing moments, pine in want, drink the salt tear; their morsel, the bread of misery, whilst shrinking from the cold blast into their cheerless hovels.
  Re-enter **Banks**, *leading in* **Amelia**.

Banks: Madam, my sister. *(Bows and retires)*

Lady Amaranth: Friend thou art welcome—I feel myself interested in thy concerns.

Amelia: Madam!

51

Lady Amaranth: I judge thou wert not always unhappy—Tell me thy condition, then I shall better know how to serve thee. Is thy brother thy sole kindred?

Amelia: I had a husband, and a son.

Lady Amaranth: A widow! If it recall not images thou wouldst forget, impart to me thy story—'Tis rumour'd in the village, thy brother is a clergyman—tell me.

Amelia: Madam, he was; but he has lost his early patron, and is now poor and unbeneficed.

Lady Amaranth: But thy husband—

Amelia: By this brother's advice, now twenty years since, I was prevailed on to listen to the addresses of a young sea officer, (my brother was then a chaplain in the navy) but to our surprise and mortification, we discovered by the honesty of a sailor, in whom he put confidence, that the Captain's design was only to decoy me into a seeming marriage, he having ordered him to procure a counterfeit clergyman; our humble friend, instead of us, put the deceit upon his master, by concealing from him that my brother was in orders; he, flattered with the hopes of procuring me an establishment, gave in to the supposed imposture, and performed the ceremony.

Lady Amaranth: Duplicity, even with a good intent, is ill.

Amelia: Madam, the event has justified your censure; for my husband, not knowing himself bound by any legal tie, abandoned me—I followed him to the Indies, distracted, still seeking him—I left my infant at one of our settlements; but, after a fruitless pursuit, on my return, I found the friend to whose care I had committed my child, was compelled to retire from the ravages of war, but where I could not learn: rent with agonising pangs, now without child or husband, I again saw England, and my brother, who, wounded with remorse, for being the cause of my misfortune, secluded himself from the joys of social life, and invited me to partake the repose of solitude in that humble asylum, from whence we've both just now been driven.

Lady Amaranth: My pity can do thee no good, yet I pity thee; but as resignation to what must be, may restore peace, if my means can procure thee comfort, they are at thy pleasure.

Come, let thy griefs subside, instead of thy cottage, accept thou and thy brother every convenience that my mansion can afford.

Amelia: Madam, I can only thank you with—*(weeps)*

Lady Amaranth: My thanks are here—thou shalt be cheerful. I will introduce thee to my sprightly cousin Harry, and his father, my humorous uncle; we have delights going forward that may amuse thee.

Amelia: Kind lady!

Lady Amaranth: Come smile—Tho' a quaker, thou seest I am merry—the sweetest joy of wealth and power is to cheer another's drooping heart, and wipe from the pallid cheek, the tear of sorrow.

Exeunt.

END OF THE FOURTH ACT

ACT FIVE

SCENE ONE

A Road.
Enter **Three Ruffians**, *dressed as sailors.*

1st Ruffian: Well, now, what's to be done?

2nd Ruffian: Why, we've been long upon our shifts, and after all our tricks, twists, and turns, as London was then too hot for us, our tramp to Portsmouth was a hit.

3rd Ruffian: Ay; but since the cash we touched, upon pretending to be able bodied seamen is now come to the last shilling, as we have deserted, means of a fresh supply to take us back to London must be thought on.

2nd Ruffian: How to recruit the pocket without hazarding the neck.

1st Ruffian: By an advertisement posted on the stocks yonder, there are highwaymen upon this road; thirty guineas are offered by the quaker lady, owner of the estate round here, to him, who shall apprehend one of these collectors; I wish we could snap up any straggler to bring before her. A quaker will only require a yea for an oath—we might sack these thirty guineas.

2nd Ruffian: Yes; but we must take care, if we fall into the hands of this gentleman that's in pursuit of us—S'death isn't that his man, the old boatswain?

1st Ruffian: Don't run, I think we three are a match for him. Instantly put on your characters of sailors, we may get something out of him; a pitiful story makes such an impression on the soft heart of a true tar, that he'll open his hard hand and drop you his last guinea—If we can but make him believe we were pressed, we have him, only mind me.

Enter **John Dory**.

John: To rattle my lantern! Sir George's temper now always blows a hurricane.

2nd Ruffian *(to* **John***)*: What cheer?

John: Ha hoy!

3rd Ruffian: Bob, up with your speaking trumpet.

2nd Ruffian: Do you see, brother, this is the thing.

Enter **Sir George**, *at the back unperceived*.

Sir George *(aside)*: If these should be my deserters.

1st Ruffian: We three hands, just come home after a long voyage, were pressed in the river, and without letting us see our friends, brought round to Portsmouth, and there we entered freely, 'cause why? We had no choice, then we run. We hear some gentleman is in chase of us, so as the shot is all out, we'll surrender.

John: Surrender! Oh then you've no shot left indeed—let's see. *(Feels his pocket)* I hav'nt the loading of a gun about me now, and this same monsieur poverty is a bitter bad enemy.

Sir George *(aside)*: They are the deserters that I've been after!

John: Meet me in an hour's time in the little wood yonder, I'll raise a wind to blow you into safe latitude—keep out to sea, my master's the rock you'll certainly split upon.

2nd Ruffian: This is the first time we ever saw you, but we'll steer by your chart, for I never knew one seaman to betray another. *Exeunt* **Ruffians**.

Sir George *(aside)*: Then they have been pressed—I can't blame them so much for running away.

John: Yes, Sir George would certainly hang 'em.

Sir George *(advancing)*: I wouldn't, they shall eat beef, and drink the King's health, run and tell them so—stop, I'll tell them myself.

John: Why, now you are yourself, and a kind, good gentleman, as you used to be.

Sir George: Since these idle rogues are inclined to return to their duty, they shan't want sea-store—take them this money—but hold—I'll meet them myself, and advise them as I would my children.

Exeunt severally.

SCENE TWO

A Wood.
Enter **Rover**, *in his first clothes, with Pistols.*

Rover *(agitated)*: Which way did Mr Abrawang take? Dick Buskin, I think, has no suspicion of my intentions:— Such a choleric spark will fight, I dare say. If I fall, or even survive this affair, I leave the field of love and the fair prize to the young man I've personated, for I'm determined to see Lady Amaranth no more—oh, here comes Abrawang.
　　Enter **Sir George**.
Sir George: Now to relieve these foolish sea-gulls—they must be hovering about this coast—Ha! puppy unknown!
Rover: You, Sir, are the very man I was seeking.—You are not ignorant, Mr Abrawang—
Sir George: Mr. What?
Rover: You will not resign your title, ha, ha, ha! Oh, very well, I'll indulge you, Sir George Thunder, you honoured me with a blow.
Sir George: Did it hurt you?
Rover: S'death! Sir, as it's my pride to reject even favours, no man shall offer me an injury.
Sir George: Eh!
Rover: In rank we're equal.
Sir George: Are we faith? The English of all this is, we're to fight.
Rover: Sir, you've marked on me an indelible stain, only to be washed out by blood.
Sir George: Why, I've only one objection to fighting you.

Rover: What's that, sir?

Sir George: That you're too brave a lad to be killed.

Rover: Brave! No, sir; at present I wear the stigma of a coward.

Sir George: Zounds! I like a bit of fighting—havn't had a morsel a long time—don't know when I've smelt gunpowder—but to bring down a woodcock.

Rover: Take your ground.

Sir George: Yes, but are we to thrust with bulrushes like two frogs, or, like squirrels, to pelt each other with nut shells? For I see no other weapons here.

Rover: Oh yes, sir; here are weapons *(gives a pistol)*

Sir George: Well, this is bold work, for a Privateer to give battle to a King's ship.

Rover: Try your charge, sir, and take your ground.

Sir George: I would not wish to sink, burn, or destroy, what I think was built for good service: but, damme, if I don't wing you to teach you better manners. *(rams the charge)*
> *Enter the* **Three Ruffians**, *not perceiving* **Rover**.

3rd Ruffian *(looking at* **Sir George***)*: Ay, here's the honest fellow has brought us some cash.

2nd Ruffian: We're betrayed, it's the very man that's in pursuit of us; and this promise was only a decoy to throw us into his power—The pistol! *(apart and pointing to it)*. We'll secure you *(seizes and wrenches the pistol from* **Sir George***)*.

Sir George: Ah, boys!

2nd Ruffian: You'd have our lives, now we'll have yours.
> *Presents the piece at* **Sir George**. **Rover** *advances, and knocks it out of his hand.*
> *They run off.*

Rover: Rascals! *(pursues them)*

Sir George *(takes up the other pistol)*: My brave lad! I'll—*(going)*
> *Enter* **John Dory**.

John: No, you sha'nt. *(holding him)*

Sir George: The rogues will—

John: Never mind the rogues—
> *Noise of fighting without, a shot fired.*

Sir George: S'blood! Must I see my preserver perish. *(struggling)*

John: Well, I know I'm your preserver, and I will perish, but I'll bring you out of harm's way. *(Still holding him)*

Sir George: Though he'd fight me himself—

John: Sure we all know you'd fight the devil.

Sir George: He saved my life.

John: I'll save your life. *(Takes him in his arms)* So hey! haul up, my noble little crab walk!

> *Exit.*

SCENE THREE

A Room in Bank's Cottage.
Enter **Farmer Gammon, Banks** *and* **Sim**—*(Sim writing and crying).*

F. Gammon: Boy, go on with the inventory.

Sim *(aside)*: How unlucky! Feyther to lay hold of me when I wanted to practice my part.

Banks: This proceeding is very severe, to lay an execution on my wretched trifling goods.

F. Gammon: Ay, you know you've gone up to the big house with your complaint—her ladyship's steward, to be sure, has made me give back your cottage, and farm; but your goods I seize for my rent.

Banks: Only leave me a very few necessaries—by the goodness of my neighbours, I may soon redeem what the law has put into your hands.

F. Gammon: The affair is now in my lawyer's hands, and plaintiff and defendant chattering about it, is all smoke.

Sim: Feyther, don't be so cruel to Mr Banks.

F. Gammon: I'll mark what I may want to keep for myself. *(to Sim)* Stay here and see that not a pin's worth be removed without my knowledge. *(Exit)*

Sim: I'll be dom'd if I'll be your watchdog to bite the poor, that I won't. Mr Banks, as feyther intends to put up your goods at auction, if you could but get a friend to buy the choice of them for you again. Sister Jane has got steward to advance her a quarter's wages, and when I've gone to sell corn for feyther, besides presents, I've made a market penny now and then.

Here—it's not much; but every little helps. *(Takes out a small leather purse, and offers it to* **Banks***.)*

Banks: I thank you, my good-natured boy; but keep your money.

Sim: Last summer, you saved me from being drown'd in black pool, if you'll not take this. Ecod, in there I'll directly fling it, and let old nick save it, from being drowned, an' he can; take it—now do take it—take it—take it. *(weeps)*

Banks: My kind lad, then I'll not hurt your feeling by opposing your liberality. *(Takes it)*

Sim: He, he, he! you've now given my heart such a pleasure as I never felt, nor I'm sure feyther afore me.

Banks: But, Sim, whatever may be his opinion of worldly prudence, still remember he's your parent.

Sim: I will—'One elbow chair, one claw table'.

Exeunt **Sim** *writing.*

Enter **Amelia.**

Amelia: The confusion into which Lady Amaranth's family is thrown by the sudden departure, and apprehended danger of her young cousin, must have prevented her ladyship from giving that attention to our affairs, that I'm sure was her inclination. If I can but prevail on my brother too, to accept her protection—I can't enjoy the delights of her Ladyship's hospitable mansion, and leave him here still subject to the insults of the churlish farmer—Heavens! who's this? *(Retires)*

Enter **Rover,** *hastily, his hair and dress disordered.*

Rover: What a race! I've at last got from the blood-hounds! Ah, if old Abrawang had but followed and backed me, we'd have 'tickled their catastrophes'; but when they got me alone, three upon one were odds, so, safe's the word: What did they want with my life, if printed, it wouldn't sell for sixpence. Who's house is this I've dash'd into?—Eh! the friendly cottage of my old gentleman, are you at home? *(calls)* Gadso! I had a hard struggle for it; yes, murder was their intent, so it was well for me that I was born without brains, I'm quite weak, faint! *(Leans against the wall)*

Amelia *(advancing)*: Sir, are not you well? *(With concern)*

Rover: Madam, I ask pardon—hem, yes ma'am very well, I thank you—now exceeding well—got into an affray there, a kind of hobble with some worthy gentlemen; only simple, honest farmers. I fancy mistook me for a sheaf of barley, for they down with me, and then thresh'd so heartily, gad, their flails flew merrily about my ears, but I up, and when I could no longer fight like a mastiff, why, I ran like a greyhound—But, dear, ma'am, pray excuse me. This is very rude, faith.

Amelia: You seem disturbed, Sir, will you take any refreshment?

Rover: Madam, you're very good.—Only a little of your currant wine, if you please; if I don't forget it stands—just *(points, Amelia brings a decanter from a beaufet, Rover takes it and fills)* Madam, I've the honour of drinking your health. *(Drinks)*

Amelia: I hope you're not hurt, Sir.

Rover: 'A little better, but very faint still',—I had a sample of this before, and liked it so much, that, madam, 'Won't you take another?'

Amelia: Sir! *(takes a glass and lays it by)*

Rover: Madam, 'if you'd been fighting, as I have', you'd—well, well, *(Fills and drinks)* now I'm as well as any man—'In Illyria', got a few hard knocks tho'.

Amelia: You'd better repose a little, you seemed much disordered coming in.

Rover *(places chairs and both sit)*: Why, ma'am, you must know, thus it was—

> *Enter* **Sheriff's Officer.**

Officer: Come, ma'am, Mr Gammon says this chair is wanted to make up the half dozen above.

> *Lays hold of* **Amelia**'s *chair, she rises terrified.*

Rover: What, what's all this?

Officer: Why, the furniture's seized on execution, and a man must do his duty.

Rover: Then, scoundrel, know, a man's first duty is civility and tenderness to a woman.

Amelia: Heavens! where's my brother? This gentleman will bring himself into trouble.

Officer: Master, d'ye see, I'm representative for his honour the High Sheriff.

Rover: Every High Sheriff should be a gentleman, and when he's represented by a rascal, he's dishonoured.—Dem it, I might as well live about Covent Garden, and every night get beating the watch; for here, among groves and meadows, I'm always squabbling with constables.

Takes up a stick from a corner of the room, and holds it behind him.

Officer: Come, come, I must—

Rover: 'As you say, sir, last Wednesday, so it was,'—Sir, your most obedient humble servant *(Bows)* Pray, Sir, may I take the liberty to know, were you ever astonished?

With great ceremony.

Officer: What?

Rover: Because, Sir, I intend to astonish you; my dear fellow, give me your hand. *(Takes his hand and strikes him)* Now, Sir, you are astonished.

Officer: Yes; but see if I don't sue you with an action.

Rover: 'Right, suit the action to the word, the word to the action, see if the gentlewoman be not affrighted'—'Michael, I'll make thee an example.'

Officer: Yes, fine example, when goods are seized here by the law, and—

Rover: 'Thou worm and maggot of the law!' 'Hop me over every kennel, or you shall hop without my custom.'

Officer: I don't value your custom.

Rover: You are astonished, now I'll amaze you.

Officer: No, I won't be amazed—but only see if I don't—

Rover: Hop. *(Exit* **Officer** *muttering and frightened.)* Stop ma'am, these sort of gentry are unpleasant company for a lady—So I'll just see him to the door, and then I'll see him outside the door. Ma'am, I'm your most obedient humble servant. *(Bows and exits hastily)*

Amelia: I feel a strange curiosity to know who this young gentleman is. He must have known the house by the freedom—but then his gaiety, (without familiar rudeness) native elegance of manners, and good breeding, seem to make him at home any where—My brother, I think must know—

Enter **Banks***, hastily, and agitated.*

Banks: Amelia, did you see the young man that was here? Some ruffians and a posse of the country people have bound and dragged him from the door, on the allegation of three men who mean to swear he has robbed them. They have taken him to Lady Amaranth's.

Amelia: How! He did enter here in confusion as if pursued; but I'll stake my life on his innocence.

Banks: The freedom of his censures on Farmer Gammon's conduct, and the friendly office he did me, have brought the sordid churl's malice on him, and he has encouraged these ruffians, in hopes of the reward offered by Ephraim Smooth, for apprehending foot pads, to drag the young fellow up to Lady Amaranth's, where the Farmer says, he has already appear'd in a feign'd character.

Amelia: I'll speak to Lady Amaranth, and in spite of calumny, he shall have justice—he would not let me be insulted, because he saw me an unprotected woman, without a husband or a son, and shall he want an advocate? Brother, come.

Exeunt.

SCENE FOUR; AND LAST

A dressing room in **Lady Amaranth**'s.
Enter **Jane**, *with a light.*

Jane: I believe there's not a soul in the house but myself; my lady has sent all the folks round the country to search after the young 'squire, she'll certainly break her heart if any thing happens to him; I don't wonder, for surely he's a dear, sweet gentleman, the pity of it is, his going spoils all our fine play, and I had just got my part quite by heart; however, I must do the room up for Mr Banks' sister, that my lady has invited here. *(Adjusts the toilet).*

    Enter **Ephraim Smooth**.

Ephraim: The man, John Dory, has carried the man George, hither in his arms, and has locked him up. Coming into the house, they did look to me like a blue lobster with a shrimp in his claws—Oh, here is the damsel I love, and alone.

Jane: They say when folks look in the glass, at night, they can see the black gentleman.

    As she's looking in the glass, sees **Ephraim** *over her shoulder, screams.*

Ephraim: Thou art employ'd in vanity.

Jane: Well, who want's you?

Ephraim: It is natural for woman to love man.

Jane: Yes; but not such ugly men as you. Why would you come in to frighten me, when you know there's nobody here but ourselves.

Ephraim: I am glad of that. I am the elm and thou the honeysuckle; let thy arms entwine me.

64

Jane *(aside)*: Oh, what a rogue is here! but yonder comes my lady, and I'll show him off to her in his true colours.

Ephraim: Clasp me around.

Jane: Well, I will, if you'll take off your hat, and make me a fine low bow.

Ephraim: I cannot bend my knee, nor take off my beaver.

Jane: Then you're very impudent—go along.

Ephraim: But to win thy favour. *(takes off his hat and bows)*

Jane: Now kneel down to me.

Ephraim: I cannot, but one lovely smile may smile me down.

 She smiles, he kneels.

Jane: Well now, read me a speech out of that fine play book.

Ephraim: I read a play! a-bo-mi-na-ti-on!—But, Jane, wilt thou kiss me?

Jane: I kiss a man!—a-bo-mi-na-ti-on! But you may take my hand—

Ephraim: Oh! tis a comfort to the lip of the faithful *(Kisses her hand)*

 Enter **Lady Amaranth**.

Lady Amaranth: How! *(Taps him on the shoulder).* Ah, thou sly and deceitful hypocrite!

Jane: There, ma'am is the demure, holy man that would prevent our play.

Lady Amaranth: So severely censure others, and put fetters on me, which now I'm determined to break.

Ephraim: Verily Mary, I was buffeted by Satan in the shape of a damsel.

Lady Amaranth: Go.

Ephraim: My spirit is sad, tho' my feet move so nimble. *(Exit slowly)*

Lady Amaranth: But, Oh, heavens, no tidings of my dearest Henry! Jane, let them renew their search.

Jane: Here's Madam Amelia, you see I've got her room ready, my lady, but I'll go make brother Sim look for the young 'squire. *(Exit)*

 Enter **Amelia**.

Amelia: Oh, madam, might I implore your influence with—

Lady Amaranth: Friend, thou art ill accomodated here, but I hope thou wilt excuse—My mind is a sea of trouble, my peace shipwrecked—Oh, friend hadst thou seen my cousin Harry, thou too, all who knew him, must be anxious for his safety. How unlucky this servant to prevent Sir George from giving him that assistance, which paternal care, and indeed gratitude demanded, for it was filial affection which led him to pursue those wicked men.

John *(without)*: Heave a-head.

    Enter **John Dory**, *and* **Sir George**.

Sir George: Rascal! Whip me up like a pound of tea, dance me about like a young bear, make me quit the preserver of my life! yes, puppy unknown will think me a poltroon, and that I was afraid to follow, and second him.

John: Well, you may as well turn into your hammock for this night out you shall not budge. *(sees* **Amelia***)* Oh! mercy of heaven! isn't it—Eh, master? Only give one look.

Amelia *(seeing* **Sir George***)*: My husband!

    Swoons; **Lady Amaranth** *supports her.*

Sir George: Tis my Amelia!

John *(stopping* **Sir George***, and looking attentively at* **Amelia***)*: Reef the foresail! first, you crack'd her heart by sheering off, and now you'll overset her by bringing to.—

Lady Amaranth: Hold—soft! She recovers.

Amelia: Are you at length returned to me, my Seymour?

Lady Amaranth: Seymour! Her mind is disturbed, this is mine uncle, Sir George Thunder.

John: No, no, my lady, she knows what she's saying very well.

Sir George: Niece, I have been a villain to this lady, I confess. But, my dear Amelia, Providence has done you justice in part. From the first month I quitted you, I have never entered one happy hour on my journal; hearing that you foundered and considering myself the cause, the worm of remorse has since gnawed my timbers.

Amelia: You're not still offended with me.

Sir George: Me! if you can forgive my offence, and condescend to take my hand as an atonement? ·

Amelia: Your hand! Do you forget that we are already married?

Sir George: Ay, there was my rascality.

John: You may say that.

Sir George: That marriage, my dear—I'm asham'd to own it;

but it was—

John: As good as if you had been lash'd together by the chaplain of the Eagle.

Sir George: Hold your tongue, you impudent crimp, you pandar, you bad adviser,—I'll strike my false colours, I now acknowledge the chaplain you provided was—

John: Was a good man, and a greater honour to his black, than your honour has been to your blue cloth—Eh, by the word of a seaman, here he is himself.

Enter **Banks**.

Sir George: Your brother?

Banks: Captain Seymour!

Sir George: My dear Banks, I'll make every reparation—Amelia shall really be my wife.

Banks: That, Sir, my sister is already; for when I performed the marriage ceremony, which you took only as the cloak of your deception, I was actually in orders.

John: Now, who's the crimp, and the pandar? I never told you this since; because I thought a man's own reflections were the best punishment for betraying an innocent woman.

Sir George: You shall be a post-captain, sink me, if you shan't—*(shakes hands with* **John Dory***)*.

Lady Amaranth: Madam, my inmost soul partaketh of thy gladness, and joy for thy reformation. *(To* **Sir George***)* But thy prior marriage to this lady, annuls the subsequent, and my cousin Harry is not now thy heir.

Sir George: So much the better; he's an unnatural cub; but, Amelia, I flatter myself I have an heir, my infant boy—

Amelia: Ah, husband, you had.

Sir George: Gone! well, well, I see I have been a miserable scoundrel—Eh, I will, yes, if my son Harry proceeds in his unworthy disobedience, I'll adopt that brave, kind lad, that wouldn't let any body kill me but himself. He shall have my estate, that's my own acquisition—My lady, marry him, puppy unknown's a fine fellow! Amelia, only for him, you would never have found your husband Captain Seymour, in Sir George Thunder.

Amelia: How!

Banks: Are you Sir George Thunder?

John: Oh, I didn't tell you that at the time because you might be for finding him out too soon and upstall.

Enter **Landlord**, *followed by* **Ephraim Smooth**.

Landlord: Please you, Madam, they've got a footpad in custody.

Ephraim: I am come to sit in judgment, for there is a bad man in thy house, Mary.

John: Then why don't you get out of it.

Ephraim: Bring him before me.

Sir George: Before you, old squintibus! And perhaps you don't know I'm a magistrate?

Ephraim: I'll examine him.

Sir George: You be damn'd—I'll examine him myself. *(shoves* **Ephraim***)*. Tow him in here. I'll give him a passport to Winchester bilboes.

Amelia *(kneels to* **Sir George***)*: Oh, Sir, as you hope for mercy, extend it to this youth; but even should he be guilty, which from our knowledge of his benevolent and noble nature, I think next to an impossibility, let the services he has rendered to us—he protected, relieved your forsaken wife, and her unhappy brother, in the hour of want and sorrow.

Sir George: What, Amelia, plead for a robber! Consider, my love, justice is above bias or partiality. If my son violated the laws of his country, I'd deliver him up a public victim to disgrace and punishment.

Lady Amaranth: Ah, my impartial uncle! Had thy country any laws to punish him, who instead of paltry gold, would rob the artless virgin of her dearest treasure, in the rigid Judge, I should now behold the trembling criminal.

Enter **Twitch**, *with* **Rover** *bound, who keeps his face averted, and* **Two Ruffians**.

Ephraim *(advances)*: Speak thou.

Sir George: Hold thy clapper thou.—Who are the prosecutors?

Ephraim: Call in—

Sir George: Will nobody stop his mouth.

John Dory *pushes* **Ephraim** *against the wall*.

Who are the prosecutors?

Twitch: There, tell his worship, the Justice.

2nd Ruffian: A Justice—Oh! the devil! *(aside)* I thought we should have nothing but quakers to deal with.

Sir George: Come, how did this fellow rob you?

2nd Ruffian: Why, your honour, I'll swear—*(in a feigned country voice)*

Sir George *(Looking at them)*: Oh, ho!

2nd Ruffian: Zounds, we're wrong—this is the very—

Sir George: Clap down the hatches, secure these sharks.

Rover: I thought I should find you here, Abrawang, and that you had some knowledge of these fellows.

Lady Amaranth *(aside)*: Heavens! my cousin Harry—

Sir George: The devil! isn't this my spear and shield?

John *(advances)*: My young master—Oh! what have you been at here? This rope may yet be wanted. *(Unbinds Rover)*

    Enter **Harry.**

Harry: My dear fellow, are you safe?

Rover: Yes, Dick, I was brought in here very safe, I assure you.

Harry: A confederate in custody below has made a confession of their villainy, that they concerted this plan to accuse him of a robbery, first, for revenge, then, in hopes to share the reward for apprehending him; he also owns they are not sailors, tho' they fraudulently took the bounty, but depredators on the public.

Sir George: Keep them safe in limbo.

    The **Ruffians** *taken off.*

Sir George: Not knowing that the Justice of Peace whom they've brought the lad now here before, is the very man they attacked, ha, ha, ha! The rogues have fallen into their own snare.

Rover: What, now, you're a Justice of the Peace? Well said, Abrawang!

Amelia: Then, Sir George you know him too?

Sir George: Know puppy unknown! to be sure.

Rover: Still, Sir George! What, then, you will not resign your knighthood? *(to* **Amelia***)* Madam, I am happy to see you again. *(Shakes hands with* **Banks***)*—Ah, how do you do, my kind host?

Lady Amaranth: I rejoice at thy safety—*(to* **Sir George***)* Be reconciled to him.

Sir George: Reconciled!—If I don't love, respect and honour him, I should be unworthy of the life he rescued. But who is he?

Harry: Sir, he is—

Rover: Dick, I thank you for your good wishes; but I am determined not to impose on this lady—Madam, as I at first told this well meaning tar, when he forced me to your house, I am not the son of Sir George Thunder.

John: No! Then I wish you were the son of an admiral, and I your father.

Harry: You refuse the lady! To punish you I've a mind to take her myself.—My dear cousin—

Rover: Stop, Dick.—If I who adore her won't, you shall not. No, no; Madam, never mind what this fellow says, he's as poor as myself—Isn't he Abrawang?

Harry: Then, my dear Rover, since you are so obstinately disinterested, I'll no longer tease my father, whom you here see, and in your strolling friend, his very truant Harry, that ran from Portsmouth school, and joined you and fellow comedians.

Rover: Indeed!

Harry *(to* **Lady Amaranth***)*: Dear cousin, forgive me, if thro' my zeal for the happiness of my friend, I endeavoured to promote yours, by giving you a husband more worthy than myself.

Rover: Am I to believe! Madam, is your uncle, Sir George Thunder, in this room?

Lady Amaranth: He is. *(Looking at* **Sir George***)*.

Rover: 'Tis so! you in reality, what I've had the impudence to assume! and have perplexed your father with my ridiculous effrontery.— *(Turns to* **John Dory***, angrily)* I told you, I insisted I wasn't the person you took me for, but you would thrust me into your chariot and drag me hither. I am ashamed, and mortified, Madam, I take my leave—

Ephraim: Thou art welcome to go.

Rover *(apart)*: Sir George, as the father of my friend, I cannot lift my hand against you; but I hope Sir, you'll apologise to me.

Sir George: Ay, with pleasure my noble splinter—Now tell me from what dock you were launched, my heart of oak?

Rover: I've heard, in England, Sir; but from my earliest knowledge, till within a very few years, I've been in the East

Indies.

Sir George: Beyond seas? Well, and how?

Rover: It seems I was committed an infant to the care of a lady, who was herself obliged by the gentle Hyder Ally, to strike her toilet, and decamp without beat of drum, leaving me a chubby little fellow, squatted on a carpet. A serjeant's wife alone, returned, and snatched me off triumphant, thro' fire, smoke, cannon, cries and carnage.

Lady Amaranth *(to* **Amelia***)*: Dost thou mark?

Amelia: Sir, can you recollect the name of the town, where—

Rover: Yes, ma'am, the town was Negapatnam.

Amelia: I thank you, Sir. *(Gazes with delight and earnestness on* **Rover***)*.

Rover: An officer, who'd much rather act Scrub on the stage, than Hotspur in the field, brought me up behind the scenes on the Calcutta theatre—I was rolled on the boards, acted myself into the favour of a colonel, promised a pair of colours; but, impatient to find my parents, hid myself in the steerage of an homeward bound ship, assumed the name of Rover from the uncertainty of my fate, and having murdered more poets than Rajahs, stept on English ground, unencumbered with rupees or pagodas. Ha, ha! wouldst thou come home so, little Ephraim?

Ephraim: I would bring myself home with some money.

Amelia: Excuse my curiosity, Sir, what was the lady's name in whose care you were left?

Rover: Oh, ma'am she was the lady of a Major Linstock; but I heard my mother's name was Seymour?

Sir George: Why, Amelia?

Amelia: My son!

Rover: Madam!

Amelia: It is my Charles! *(Embraces him)*

Sir George: Eh!

Lady Amaranth: Thou seest he is my gay, gallant, generous cousin—

John: Tol, lol, lol, tho' I never heard it before, my heart told me he was a chip of the old block.

Amelia *(to* **Rover,** *pointing to* **Sir George***)*: —Your father!—

Rover: Can it? Heaven! then have I attempted to raise my impious nand against a parent's life!

Sir George: My dear brave boy! My son with spirit to fight me as a stranger, yet defend me as a father.

Amelia: And knowing her only as a woman wronged, to protect his helpless mother.

Banks: By relieving the stranger, Charles, you little thought 'twas an uncle you snatched from a prison.

Lady Amaranth: Nor that thou by that benign action, did first engage the esteem of thy fond cousin, *(takes him by the hand)*, Uncle, you'll recollect 'twas I, who first introduced a son to thee,

Sir George: And I hope you will next introduce a grandson to me, young slyboots. Harry you've lost your fortune.

Harry: Yes, Sir, but I've gained a brother, whose friendship (before I knew him to be such) I prized above any fortune in England.

Rover: My dearest Rosalind!

Amelia *(to* **Lady Amaranth***)*: Then, will you take our Charles?

Lady Amaranth: Yes: but only on condition thou bestowest thy fortune on his friend and brother, mine is suffiient for us, is it not?

Rover: Angelic creature! to think of my generous friend—But now for 'As You Like It'. Where's Lamp and Trap—I shall ever love a play—a spark from Shakespeare's Muse of Fire was the star that guided me thro' my desolate and bewildered maze of life, and brought me to these unexpected blessings.

'To merit friends so good, so sweet a wife,

The tender husband be my part for life;

My Wild Oats sown, let candid Thespian Laws

Decree that glorious harvest—your applause.'

THE END

THE LIFE OF JOHN O'KEEFFE

by
Clifford Williams

'I was born in Abbey-street, Dublin, on the 24th June, 1747; my father was a native of the King's County, and my mother of the county of Wexford.' Thus begins O'Keeffe's *Recollections* published eighty years later in 1826. As a child he studied drawing at Mr West's Dublin Royal Academy, and learnt Greek, Latin and French at Father Austin's school on Cook-street. He read Shakespeare, Ben Jonson, Congreve and Farquhar. The first edition of Farquhar's comedies set him studying and acting plays with his schoolfellows. His first visit to the theatre was at the age of eight when he saw Peg Woffington play Alicia in *Jane Shore*.

In 1762, he went to London for the first time, residing with an uncle and aunt in Cleveland-row for two years. He roamed round London, drew a great deal, went to the theatre (he saw Garrick as Lear), and wrote his first play—a five act comedy *The Generous Lovers*. The play was never performed and the MS lost. Back in Dublin in 1764, he wrote a second play—a two act drama *The She Gallant*. This was produced by the tragedian Mossop (Henry) at his Smock Alley Theatre. O'Keeffe joined Mossop's company as an actor, playing in Dublin and the provinces. He continued drawing and he wrote poetry. He acted comic parts in the main, and the fate of a fellow actor Mahon who, tho' a comedian, essayed to play a tragic tyrant, prompted O'Keeffe to the following verses (Mahon, in 'dying' upon the carpet—it was the custom for a carpet to be carried on for the hero to die upon—had become inextricably caught up in the 'tragic tablecloth' to the audience's mirth):

73

Stranger:
Why let the wounded man lie bleeding there,
Flouncing and gasping, like a new-caught sturgeon?
And why not place him in an easy chair,
And some one run and fetch the nearest surgeon?

Play-goer:
Sir,'tis his part upon the stage to lie:
In acting up to nature, none goes higher.
We come on purpose, sir, to see him die;
And paid our cash—he's such a lovely dier!

The verses are no great shakes, but they were apparently impromptu. In any case, O'Keeffe's final word on the subject is masterly—'We of the comic light infantry may be allowed to fling a jest now and then at the tragic heavy horse'.

O'Keefe married Mary Heaphy in 1774. They had three children. Gerald, who died in infancy, John Tottenham and Adelaide. He decided to support his family in writing plays, tho' in the same year his eyesight began to deteriorate. His farce *Tony Lumpkin In Town* (a sequel to Goldsmith's *She Stoops To Conquer*) had been produced in Dublin in 1773. He brushed it up and sent it to George Colman Sen. who was Patentee of the Theatre Royal Haymarket in London. In 1778 the play was produced with some success, and Colman was keen on further plays from O'Keeffe. O'Keeffe was delighted. 'I determined to follow the trumpet of Fame, and the rattling music of Fortune's purse, by my new London finger-post,—my dramatic pen.'

In 1779, Colman produced O'Keeffe's next play *The Son-in-Law* which was a triumph. O'Keeffe uprooted himself from Ireland and sailed to England for the last time in 1781. He had already supplied Colman with a further two act play—*Dead Alive*, based on a story in the *Arabian Nights*. Now, he settled in lodgings in Macclesfield Street next door to his brother Daniel (an eminent miniature painter) and wrote one of his best-known plays—*The Agreeable Surprise*. It was the last he wrote in his own hand for his eyesight continued to fail. Charles Macklin, the famous Shylock of the 18th Century, saw the first performance and was heard to remark as the curtain fell—'*The Agreeable Surprise* is the best farce in the English language except the *Son in Law.'*

Thomas Harris, the Covent Garden Theatre proprietor and manager, asked O'Keeffe for an opera. O'Keeffe was ill and tired, and tried to delay its writing. But Harris wanted it before Christmas. O'Keeffe responded with his habitual willingness and generosity. 'I worked hard and terrified was I at the voice of the evening muffin-man at three o'clock, at having done no more that day.' The piece, *The Banditti, or Love's Labyrinth*, was completed on time, and was a total failure. 'Before the curtain dropped on my defeat I slipped out of the theatre, told my servant to call a coach, flung myself into it, and got to my lodgings, and in a state of confusion and utter despondency threw myself on the bed. I thought of my poor children, and the pang went to my heart.' The next morning Thomas Harris called on O'Keeffe. 'Mr Harris, with the greatest kindness, took all the cause of the failure on himself; said he had hurried me in the writing; that to serve the theatre I had produced the opera three months before the time agreed upon for its coming out; that he found my reputation as a dramatic author high with the public, and the temporary hurt it had suffered that night proceeded from my alacrity and industry to accomodate and oblige him.'

O'Keeffe went to Margate to convalesce, but there managed to revise *The Banditti*, write a harlequinade *Lord Mayor's Day, or a Flight from Lapland*, turn his youthful *She Gallant* into an opera—*The Positive Man*, and to complete his most famous piece—the comic opera *The Castle of Andalusia*. This was produced successfully at the Covent Garden Theatre in 1782.

The following year, O'Keeffe moved to a house in Acton. He had a large garden with an arbour in one corner. There he established himself at a marble table with John, his amanuensis, and dictated the plays and operas which were to flow continuously over the next few years—*The Young Quaker*, *The Definitive Treaty* (a *political* drama!), *The Poor Soldier*, *Friar Bacon*, *Peeping Tom*, *Fontainebleu, or Our Way in France*, and *Love in a Camp*.

He moved to Barnes, and then to Charlotte Street. His grand spectacle *Omai* was staged at Covent Garden on the 20 December, 1785, with music by Shield. *Omai* had 'incidents, characters, &, appropriate to the newly-discovered islands in the southern hemisphere, and closing with the apotheosis of Captain Cook.' The dresses and scenery were made after the drawing of Mr Webber who had accompanied Cook. Loutherbourg designed the scenery. *The Siege of Curzola* followed, then *The Man Milliner*, ('dismissed by the audience as soon as the curtain rose—not a word was heard' reports O'Keeffe), *The Farmer, Tantara-rara Rogues All, The Prisoner at Large*, *The Highland Reel*, *The Toy* (O'Keeffe's unfavourite piece), and *Aladdin, or The Wonderful Lamp*. The last four were produced in the season of 1788/89. O'Keeffe comments—'Dryden could not furnish the theatre with one play a year; therefore, though no Dryden, I may be allowed, at least to exult on the score of industry—to get a little ready money.'

O'Keeffe's next play *The Grenadier* went into rehearsal. O'Keeffe—'The world was now full of political changes in France, of which, before they rose to such horrors, people of good sense, humane intentions, and perfect friends to monarchy, did not think much amiss; and I was induced to work upon the subject of *The Man In The Iron Mask* . . . My son Tottenham [then studying in Paris—Ed] had seen the cannon go by to batter the Bastile, and heard the terrific explosions, and the appalling shouts of the people. He and the Abbé [Tottenham's tutor—Ed] were ear and eye-witnesses of many of the circumstances which I brought into this piece of mine, called *The Grenadier*. I gave it this name from Dubois, the grenadier of the National Guard, having been the first to mount the wall and enter the Bastile; but when the flame of liberty in Paris seemed to be converted into hell-fire, and patriotic men into demons, Mr Harris very prudently thought it advisable not to touch upon the subject.' The production was stopped.

O'Keeffe wrote instead a three-act opera *The Czar Peter* which included some music by Handel, then *The Loyal Bandeau*, *The Basket-Maker* and *Wild Oats*. This last comedy was presented at Covent Garden Theatre on 16 April 1791, with O'Keeffe's old friend William Lewis in the role of Rover, the travelling player whose conversation is a patchwork of quotations from other plays.

O'Keeffe received 450 guineas for *Wild Oats*. Between 1791 and 1796 he wrote further pieces for Covent Garden and the

Haymarket including *The London Hermit*, *Sprigs of Laurel*, *The World Is A Village*, *The Irish Mimic*, *Olympus in an Uproar*. In 1796 he ventured for the first time into the Drury Lane Theatre where his five-act comedy *She's Eloped* was given for one night. 'This was the last appearance of my muse before an English public. My racer that had so often started for and won the plate, and had been distanced only once *(The Man Milliner)* quitted the course to turn into the green paddock, there to walk at this leisure and lie down at his ease.'

The paddock was not particularly green! He managed to publish a collected edition of his plays in 1798—selling them by subscription. In the same year he became totally blind. He continued to write plays but they were not performed, and he found himself in difficult financial circumstances. He was given a benefit night at Covent Garden under the patronage of the Prince of Wales in 1800, and the same theatre paid him an annuity of 20 guineas from 1803 onwards. In 1804, his son Tottenham died in Jamaica where he had gone as chaplain to the Duke of Clarence. The year 1808 added a small pension from the Treasury to his meagre income.

O'Keeffe and his daughter Adelaide retired to Chichester in 1815. In early 1826, George IV granted him an annual pension of one hundred guineas, and later that year his *Recollections* were published, which he dedicated to the King.

His last home was at Southampton to which he retired in 1830. He wrote some poems there, and Adelaide read him the novels of Sir Walter Scott. In *St. Ronan's Well*, Scott had written 'From Shakespeare to O'Keeffe!' O'Keeffe remarked 'Ah! the top and the bottom of the ladder; he might have shoved me a few sticks higher'. He died at Bedford Cottage, Southampton, on 4 February, 1833, aged 85.

O'KEEFFE AND HIS CRITICS

In his *Recollections*, O'Keeffe writes—'Perhaps I may not be accused of much vanity when I state that Sheridan often gave his full opinion, that I was the first that turned the public taste from the dullness of sentiment, into which it was rapidly falling, towards the sprightly channel of comic humour; and that I was the only one that could do this. The elder Colman also declared that no dramatic author had equal power over their audience as I had. I may be proud when two such poets as the above plead for me.'

Sheridan, who managed Drury Lane Theatre from 1776 to 1809, as well as writing *The School for Scandal*, and George Colman, initially Sheridan's opposite number at the Haymarket Theatre (and author with Garrick of *The Clandestine Marriage*) were clearly men whose good opinions were feathers in O'Keeffe's cap. William Hazlitt went further. For him, O'Keeffe was 'our English Molière. The scale of the modern writer was smaller but the spirit is the same. In light, careless laughter, and pleasant exaggerations of the humours we have had no one equal to him. There is no labour or contrivance in his scenes, but the drollery of his subject seems to strike irresistibly upon his fancy and run away with his discretion as it does with ours. He is himself a Modern Antique. His fancy has all the quaintness and extravagance of the old writers. And the ease and lightness which the moderns arrogate to themselves. All his pieces are delightful.'

Later critics were not so kind. Dutton Cook wrote in 1873—'His fame has no doubt suffered on account of his fertility. He wrote in all some seventy plays, the great majority being hastily contrived to serve some temporary purpose of the managers and disappearing very shortly after their first performance . . . O'Keeffe had been an actor, and his plays fully disclose his intimate acquaintance with stage artifices of all kinds. He was bent on amusing his audience and obtaining their applause at any cost. With this view he pressed much extravagance, sham sentiment, and patriotic clap-trap into his service . . . Still he was humorous and inventive, he possessed a keen eye for character, could write very lively dialogue, and was able to provide the actors of his time with most effective occupation.'

It is possible, however, that the views expressed above may be reconciled. O'Keeffe was certainly prolific, and one can sense the tremendous pressures under which he worked: keen to oblige managements, fearful not to lose the smallest opportunity of augmenting his income, struggling to support his family, plagued by his failing eyesight, obliged to dictate his plays to an amanuensis. But there is ample proof that he took great pains over his writing, researched his subjects in depth, constantly busied himself with revision and rewriting, and generally worked with more than average courage and dedication. Moreover, from his boyhood he had been steeped in the theatre and was not 'academic' in his approach. He knew and loved) the actors for whom he wrote, and he had the advantage of sympathetic confrères in every branch of the theatre. He needed to write quickly but he was also *able* to write quickly.

Dutton Cook is right in suggesting that many of O'Keeffe's works were hastily contrived, but one must add that that would not be for the first time in the history of dramatic literature. He is less accurate in his assertion that the plays 'disappeared after their first performance'. Many of O'Keeffe's plays enjoyed very long runs by contemporary standards, and were frequently revived. There seems to be little doubt that the majority were popular and greatly captivated their audiences. But here Colman's remark must be qualified. Perhaps 'no dramatic author had equal power over their audience', but the opposition was pretty thin. The last quarter of the 18th century was not marked by the quality of its dramatists. Sheridan wrote nothing of note after *The Critic* (1779), Goldsmith died in 1774, and O'Keeffe's rivals were such writers as Richard Cumberland, Charles Pitt, and Elizabeth Inchbald, none of whom wrote anything at all memorable.

It was in a time of intensely *commercial* activity that O'Keeffe exercised his muse; he mostly worked with his back to the wall—required help to maintain a punishing 'turn-over' of plays and entertainments. That he could write a *Wild Oats*, or a *Poor Soldier* or a *Castle of Andalusia* in these circumstances, afflicted at the same time with ill health and blindness, is something of a wonder. A close inspection of *Wild Oats* will surely reveal that if O'Keeffe was not the English Molière which Hazlitt would have him, he was nevertheless a dramatist of great humour, dexterity and humanity.

Dickens celebrated him and, in particular, *Wild Oats* when Mr Cummles gives his instructions to Nicholas in *Nicholas Nickleby*—'Rover too:—you might get up Rover while you were about it, and Cassio, and Jeremy Diddler. You can easily knock them off: one part helps the other so much.'

NOTES ON THE TEXT

Wild Oats was first performed at the Covent Garden Theatre, London on 16 April 1791. O'Keeffe's plays were repeatedly printed and published surreptitiously and without his permission. They were, he said, 'full of the most glaring errors'. However, he supervised and published many of his dramatic works in an edition of five hundred copies in 1798. Each copy comprised four volumes, and *Wild Oats* is included in Volume Two, which also contained *The Wicklow Mountains, Fontaineblau, Little Hunchback, The Basket-Maker, The Blacksmith of Antwerp, The Positive Man* and *The Toy*.

The text of the present edition follows precisely that of the 1798 publication, except for the placing of the *(aside)* sign which, contrary to O'Keeffe's practice, *precedes* the words spoken in an aside.

NOTES

I.i.

John Dory and Sir George Thunder speak in nautical terms extensively (and often inaccurately) throughout the play.

Flip A warm, sweetened mixture of beer and spirits.

Dutchman A Dutch ship.

Fingered the Shot Accepted money.

Leading strings Baby reins.

The Ballad of Margaret and William A ballad by David Mallet printed in 1724, but based on a fragment on an earlier song. The ballad has many verses. The following show the song's relevance to Sir George's predicament:

> Twas at the fearful hour of midnight
> When all were fast asleep
> In glided Margaret's grimly ghost
> And stood at William's feet.
>
> Bethink thee William of thy fault
> Thy pledge and broken oath
> And give me back my maiden vow
> And give me back my troth.

Tell me of your thee's and thou's Ephraim uses the second person singular form of address as was the Quaker fashion.

Channel for the stage A boarding point for the stage-coach.

I.ii.

Enter Harry Thunder and Muz Muz was rechristened Midge in the 1791 stage production and has remained Midge subsequently.

The Academy at Portsmouth A naval school.

Colonel Standard . . . Tom Errand Characters in George Farquhar's

The Constant Couple (1699).

'*The brisk li-li-lightening*' . . . *Studying Bayes, eh, Jack?* . . . '*I am the bold Thunder*'. *The Rehearsal* (1671) by George Villiers, Duke of Buckingham, is a satire on the Heroic Play of the time. The Heroic Plays portrayed epic heroes, violent deeds and bloody events. John Dryden (1631-1700) was the greatest writer of Heroic Plays, and his *The Conquest of Granada* (1699-70) is the specific butt for Buckingham's wit. Bayes, the hero of *The Rehearsal*, is a dramatic author intent on producing his new play (he also stands for Dryden). He has written a Prologue for two characters called Thunder and Lightning.

> **Bayes:** Come out, Thunder and Lightning.
> **Thun:** I am the bold Thunder.
> **Bayes:** Mr Cartwright, pr'ythee speak a little louder, and with a hoarser voice. I am the bold Thunder? Pshaw! speak it me in a voice that thunders out indeed: I am the bold Thunder.
> **Thun:** I am the bold Thunder.
> **Light:** The brisk Lightning, I.
> **Bayes:** Nay you must be quick and nimble. The brisk Lightning, I. That's my meaning.

Harry hears Rover speaking a line from the above and assumes that Rover is rehearsing the role of Bayes. The misunderstanding which results from Harry's surname and the name of the character in Bayes' play being one and the same is a mainspring of O'Keeffe's play.

'*All in the Wrong*' The title of a comedy by Arthur Murphy, first produced at Drury Lane in 1761.

'*All around the Wrekin*' Farquhar's *The Recruiting Officer* (1706) is dedicated 'to all friends round the Wrekin'. The phrase is a traditional description for the inhabitants of Shropshire where *The Recruiting Officer* takes place. But *The Wrekin* was also the name of a London tavern in Broad Court, Bow St, frequented by O'Keeffe and his friends.

Rangers, Plumes and Foppingtons Ranger is a character in Dr. Hoadly's *The Suspicious Husband* (1747), Plume is in Farquhar's *The Recruiting Officer* and Foppington is in Vanbrugh's *The Relapse* (1696)

'*Away, the foul fiend follows me*' *King Lear*, III.iv. Edgar.

'*Ay, to foreign climates my old trunk I bear*'
Origin not discovered.

'*The Car of Thespis*' Thespis—the founder of drama—is thought to have travelled with his actors in a cart—which also served as their stage.

II.i

New scratch Wig that covered only part of the head.

'Poor Tom's a-cold' *King Lear* III.iv. Edgar.

'Hear, nature, dear Goddess . . . serpent's tooth 'tis' *King Lear*, I.iv.
Adaptation of Lear's curse on Goneril.

Drugding box A dredging-box containing flour could be used for
sprinkling over a wig.

Murrain Cattle disease.

'Madam, my master pays me . . . his commands' Farquhar, *The
Beaux' Stratagem* (1707), III. Archer, the gentleman playing the
part of a manservant, declines Mrs Sullen's tip after his song.

'Run, run Orlando . . . Unexpressive she' *As You Like It*, I.ii.
Orlando. This play was O'Keeffe's favourite Shakespearian play.

II.ii

'Yet my love indeed . . . digest as much' *Twelfth Night*, II.iv.
Orsino—garbled.

'A fig for the sultan and the Sophy' The last line of Sir Wilful
Witwood's song in Congreve's *Way of the World* (1700), IV, xi.

'Himself in one prodigious ruin'
Origin not discovered.

'I say my sister's wrong'd . . . horrible to Beedles'
Origin not discovered.

'Say that, Chamont' Chamont is the defender of his sister's honour in
Otway's *The Orphan* (1680).

'Then you are Kaskill, the angry boy?' A character in Ben Jonson's *The
Alchemist* (1610) who is described as 'the angry boy'.

'I'd kiss thee ere I kill'd thee' *Othello*, V.ii. Othello.

'No way but this, killing myself, to die upon a kiss' Ibid.

*'I've heard of your painting too: you gig, you lisp, you amble, and
nickname God's creatures'* *Hamlet*, III.i. Hamlet to Ophelia.

*'Oh that the town clerk were here, to write thee down an ass! but
though not written down in black and white, remember, thou art an
ass'* *Much Ado About Nothing*, IV.ii. Garbled Dogberry.

'Ay: to a nunnery, go' *Hamlet*, III.i. Hamlet to Ophelia.

'Tis meat and drink for me to see a clown' *As You Like It*, V.i.
Touchstone apropos William.

'Shepherd, was't ever at court?' Ibid. III.ii. Touchstone to Corin.

'Then thou art damn'd' Ibid.

'Thou art damn'd like . . . one side' Ibid.

'Your son? Young clodpate . . . teach him manners.' The reference
is to Justice Clodpate, a town-hating countryman in Thomas
Shadwell's *Epsom Wells* (1673).

'Tom Fool in King Harry' Edgar as Poor Tom in *King Lear*.

'Pillicock sat upon Pillicock Hill, Pil-i-loo, loo!' *King Lear*, III.iv.
   Edgar.

'Thou wretch! Despite o'erwhelm thee!' *Coriolanus*, III.i. Coriolanus
   to Sicinius.

'Only squint . . . tennis ball'
   Origin not discovered.

'Tho' love cool . . . 'twixt son and father' *King Lear*, I.ii. Gloucester
   on report of Edgar's treachery (mangled a little).

'Go, father . . . than his fellows' *Merchant of Venice*, II.ii Bassanio of
   Gobbo.

'Egad, it's very hard . . . gone to dinner' *The Rehearsal*. In the last act
   of this play, Bayes finds that he canot complete the rehearsal of his
   own play because the actors have gone to dinner. Rover's quotation
   is a somewhat loose one!

'Sun, moon and stars' Ibid.

'There's the sun . . . to show her tail' Ibid. Bayes has included a dance
   which shows how eclipses are produced. The character of Luna sings
   a song (including the line 'Luna means to show her tail') to the tune
   of *Tom Tyler*.

'I attend them . . . our mother' *Hamlet*, III.ii. Hamlet to Rosencrantz,
   garbled.

Rate Naval vessels were ranked according to size or 'rate'.

II.iii

Box-book
   An account of Theatre receipts.

'Sir, to return to the twenty pound'
   Origin not discovered.

Shallop A small boat. Dory means he has sent a messenger to
   Amaranth.

'But by the care of standers. by, prevented was.
   Origin not discovered.

'More music . . . twenty hautboys'
   Origin not discovered.

'Oh, such a sight! talk of a coronation'
   Origin not discovered.

'I was thinking of a side-saddle'
   Origin not discovered.

Rumbo Canakin Small drinking can for rum.

Ranger's dress Costume for role in *The Suspicious Husband* (1747)
   by Dr Hoadley.

'Cousin of Buckingham, thou sage, grave man' Richard III, III.vii.
Richard to Buckingham (with a slight change)

'Since you will buckle . . . foul faced' Ibid. Exact.

'Your mere enforcement shall acquittance me' Ibid. Exact.

Parson Palmer Thomas Fyshe Palmer. A well known 18th century cleric-preacher who was eventually transported to Australia for sedition.

'Bear me . . . for the Tigris' Nathaniel Lee, *Alexander the Great: or The Rival Queens* (1677) V.ii.

III.i

'Tis I, Hamlet the Dane' Hamlet, V.i.

'Thus far . . . marched on' Richard III, V.ii. Richmond.

'John . . . Boar'. Ibid—garbled—Richmond of Richard.

Spanish India-man Spanish vessel trading to the Indies.

'A truant disposition . . . Wirtemburg' Hamlet, I.ii. (mangled)

'Why, Ma'am, as for old Boreas . . . resentment' Partly *Henry V*, III.ii, before Harfleur, garbled.

'I think it a pity . . . save the mark' Henry IV Pt. 1. Hotspur.

'Then, Lady . . . flower' Romeo and Juliet, II.ii. Juliet, garbled.

'Excellent wench! . . . Come again' Othello, III.iii.

'If I were . . . most happy' Ibid. II.i. Othello to Desdemona.

'Let our senses . . . discord make'. As above, garbled.

'Why, you fancy . . . this family'
Origin not discovered.

'A bowl of cream . . . Majesty'
Origin not discovered.

'You get no water . . . Potentate'
Origin not discovered.

'Go, go, tho shallow Pomona'
Origin not discovered.

'The Actors . . . like to know' A Midsummer Night's Dream, V.i.
Prologue to the Pyramus and Thisbe play. Quince.

III.ii

'A bumper! A bumper of good liquor' etc. A song in Sheridan's *The Duenna* (1775).

'benefit'—I've done with benefits—Play on the word, which Harry means to refer to benefit performances at theatres.

'Fair Quaker'	*The Fair Quaker of Deal, or the Humour of the Navy'* is the title of a play by Charles Shadwell (?-1726)
'The humours of the Navy'	

Mr Buckskin Harry's name as an actor is Dick Buskin (a buskin is the high boot worn by the Greek and Roman tragic actors). John, in his anger, varies the name to 'Buckskin' which permits him to talk about currying!

IV.i

'Not the King's crown new made' Measure for Measure II. ii. Isabella.

'The Gods give us joy' As You Like It. III.iii. Spoken by Audrey to Touchstone.

Eh, what all a-mort, old Clytus A reference to Nathaniel Lee (c 1653-1692), *Alexander The Great.* Clytus is the upholder of austere virtue, as Ephraim claims to be.

'Why, you're like . . . laughing Gods' Ibid. IV.ii. But a garbled version.

'Quip and Crank . . . Hebe's cheek.' Milton *L'Allegro* (c.1631) A concert version of Milton's poem with music by Handel was often performed at the end of the 18th century.

'But I'm a Voice . . . we must' Othello I.ii. Iago to Othello. Garbled.

'By Jupiter, I swear, aye' King Lear II.ii. (misquoted, deliberately).

'You sacrilegious thief . . . thy pocket!' Hamlet. III.iv. Altered.

'Thou owl of Crete' Henry V II.i. Pistol 'O hound of Crete'.

Cuckoo's Song This comes at the end of *Love's Labours Lost,* and presumably is to be included in the Rover-Lamp *As You Like It* performance.

'Verily, I could smite . . . of the Sun''
    Origin not discovered.

Simon Pure From *A Bold Stroke for a Wife* V.i. A play (1718) by Susannah Centlivre.

Abrawang Perhaps this is a purely nonsense name. Like the gibberish Abracadabra. A wandering beggar in the 16th century—whether lunatic or feigning lunacy—was known as an Abraham-man, hence *to sham Abram* meaning to feign illness or madness.

'Quoit him down, Bardolph' Henry IV. Pt II. II.iv. Falstaff to Bardolph.

'My love more noble . . . dirty lands' Twelfth Night II.iv. Orsino.

'He's a fishmonger' Hamlet II.ii. As if Hamlet referring to Polonius.

'Motley's your only . . . the forest' As You Like It II.vii. Jaques, garbled.

'Salutation and Greeting . . . Good Audrey'. As You Like It various Touchstone phrases.

'La! Warrant what features!' As You Like It III.iii. Audrey to

Touchstone.

'*A homely thing, sir, but she's mine own*' As You Like It V.iv.
Touchstone, garbled.

'I thank the Gods for my sluttishness' *As You Like It* III.ii. Audrey,
garbled.

'*Jaffier has . . . the senate*' A reference to Otway's *Venice Preserved,
or A Plot Discovered* (1681), but not a direct quotation.

'*Ay, his conscience . . . and run*' The Merchant of Venice, II.ii. A free
snatch from Launcelot Gobbo's soliloquoy.

'*Now by my father's . . . crosses and crossed*' A loose rendition of
Petruchio to Katherine in the *Taming Of The Shrew*, IV.v.

'*And I say, as the saying is*' Ibid.

'*All the world's a stage . . .*' As You Like It II,vii. Jaques.

'*A Blow!—Essex, a blow!*'

'*Strike me . . . if I don't*' Otway *The Orphan* (1680) IV.ii. Chamont.

V.i

Pressed in the river. The press-gangs would often board homecoming
ships as they approached port and sieze sailors to man other ships. If
the sailors were allowed ashore they were all too likely to desert.

V.iii

'*In Illyria*' Twelfth Night takes place in Illyria. Refers to Sir Andrew
Aguedeek.

'*As you say, sir, last Wednesday, so it was*' Hamlet II.ii. A variation
of Hamlet's line to Polonius.

'*Right suit the action . . . not affrighted*' Hamlet III.ii. Hamlet to the
Players with echoes of Ophelia earlier.

'*Michael, I'll make thee an example*' Othello II.iii. Othello to Cassio.

'*Thou worm and maggot of the law*'
    Origin not discovered.

'*Hop me over . . . my custom*' The Taming of the Shrew IV.iii.
Petruchio to the tailor
    'Go, hop me over every kennel home,
    For you shall hop without my custom, sir:'

V.iv

'*Winchester bilboes*' The bilboes were iron bars with shackles which
confined the feet of prisoners. Thunder means Winchester jail.

'*Hyder Ally*' Hyder Ali (1722-1782), a Muslim ruler of Mysore, and
military leader against the British in India.